# Collins
# SCOTTISH
# WORDS

CW00497635

Collins

**HarperCollins Publishers**
Westerhill Road
Bishopbriggs
Glasgow
G64 2QT

www.collinslanguage.com

First Edition 2009

ISBN 978-0-00-726303-5

A–Z text © HarperCollins
Publishers 2009

Introduction © John Abernethy
2009

Illustrations © Alex Collier 2009

The moral rights of the author
have been asserted

The moral rights of the
illustrator have been asserted

Collins® is a registered
trademark of HarperCollins
Publishers Limited

A catalogue record for this book
is available from the
British Library.

Designed and typeset by
Thomas Callan

Printed in Great Britain by
Clays Ltd, St Ives plc

## Note on the Text

The list of words covered in this book is by no means an exhaustive or comprehensive list of all the words used in Scotland or of Scottish origin, but is intended to be an alphabetical compendium of the most interesting ones.

In many cases a definitive etymology of the word has been lost in time. Often a word can have more than one meaning and certainly have more than one spelling. The definitions and spellings given in this book are the ones generally considered to be the most likely and commonly accepted. Wherever possible I have mentioned alternative suggestions as to the meanings of words.

The subject of Scottish words is as rich and diverse as the people who speak it. It has its linguistic roots in Scotland's historic languages of Brythonic, Pictish, Gaelic, Norse and English and as with all living and vibrant languages, Scots is continually evolving and not stuck in a past of heritage and nostalgia. I would recommend that anyone who enjoys this book pursues further reading of Scots reference, Scots fiction, Scots poetry and Scots prose to gain an even greater understanding of both the Scots language and the Scottish people themselves.

**Editor**
Mike Munro

**Editorial Staff**
Ian Brookes
Helen Hucker
Cormac McKeown

**For the Publishers**
Lucy Cooper
Elaine Higgleton

iv

# Introduction

A few years ago, it was decided by the powers
that be that Scotland should market itself
as being The Best Small Country in the
World. This became the international slogan
for Scotland and was used extensively on
all promotional material, both at home
and abroad. The slogan was deemed to be
controversial – why was Scotland limiting
itself to being only the Best Small Country
in the World, when the title of Best Country
in the World had not officially been taken?
And furthermore why did Scotland want to
be the Best *Small* Country in the World when
there was a perfectly acceptable and common
Scots word, 'wee', that would have more
than sufficed. Why, if it was good enough for
Frank Sinatra in the 'Wee Small Hours of the
Morning' then surely it was good enough for
the Scottish tourist industry.

The history of Scotland is truly remarkable
for how much influence a small northern
region of an island on the outskirts of Europe

has had over the world. Scottish first names such as Angus, Donald and Fiona have played guitar with AC/DC, built Trump Towers and married Shrek. Scottish surnames such as MacDonald, Campbell and Stewart have become synonymous with Big Macs, tins of tomato soup and *It's A Wonderful Life*. While Scottish place names such as Perth, Hamilton and Houston have become the fourth biggest city in Australia, the capital of Bermuda, and the people you call if you have a problem in space.

As for science and inventions, where would the world be without the steam engine, the television, the telephone, penicillin, colour photography and logarithms – all invented by Scots. What about all the wonderful Scottish writers – John Buchan, Sir Walter Scott, Robert Louis Stevenson and J.M. Barrie, who have given the world *The Thirty Nine Steps*, *Rob Roy*, *Treasure Island* and *Peter Pan*. And as for December 31st, was it not the Scots who actually invented 'Hogmanay' and is it not to the words of 'Auld Lang Syne' by Scotland's national bard, Robert Burns, that millions around the world usher in the New Year? Even though most have no idea what the Scots words mean.

And wherever Scots have travelled to and settled in they have taken the Scots language with them. That wonderful historical amalgam of Pictish, Gaelic, Norse and English that is as Scottish as the land and the people that live there.

So join us on a 'dander' from the 'barry' denizens of Edinburgh and the 'gallus' folk of Glasgow, taking a detour 'doon-bye' to the Borders and Dumfries & Galloway and then, ensuring that you have first remembered to take your 'piece' with you, 'gang' north through the 'braes', 'lochs' and 'glens' of the 'couthy' Highlands, where you might spend an evening or two on the 'randan' before reaching the 'rowie' loving 'quines' and 'loons' of the North East and beyond to the 'simmer dim' of Orkney and Shetland.

On the way you may occasionally become a little 'crabbit' and even slightly 'black-affrontit' and you may be so 'scunnered' by the occasionally 'dreich' Scottish weather that you feel like having a 'greet', but by the end of the journey if previously you knew 'hee-haw' about Scottish words, you might feel slightly 'wabbit' from your exertions, but hopefully you will have been 'awfy' entertained, and 'jings, crivvens' be more conversant in the wonderful and 'weel-kent' language that is Scots. So never mind the Best Small Country in the World, be proud to be 'wee'.

Slainte mhath and lang may yer lum reek

*John Abernethy*
*2009*

## List of panels

## Pronunciation guide

Where the pronunciation of a word is unusual or of interest, guidance has been provided for the reader. The system used is self-explanatory, as far as possible, but the pronunciation guide below may be used in case of doubt.

Single vowels indicate a short sound. Longer vowels are indicated using the following letter-combinations:

| | | | |
|---|---|---|---|
| ah | as in ma | er | as in her |
| air | as in fair | oe | as in toe |
| ar | as in car | oo | as in tooth |
| aw | as in saw | or | as in for |
| ay | as in say | ow | as in how |
| i(-)e | as in mile | oy | as in boy |
| ee | as in see | uh | as in the |
| eer | as in beer | | |

Single consonants have their normal value, with other sounds being indicated by the following letter-combinations:

| | |
|---|---|
| CH | a guttural sound, as in loch |
| ch | as in chew |
| dh | a soft sound, as in they |
| sh | as in show |
| th | as in thing |
| wh | an aspirated sound, like 'hw' |

Readers should note that the letter 'r' is sounded when it follows a vowel in words such as 'for', and so the words 'sore' and 'saw' are pronounced differently in Scots, whereas an English speaker would make them sound the same.

# A–Z of Scottish Words

**agley** or **aglee** *adverb, adjective* squint, askew or wrong: *The best laid schemes o' mice an' men gang aft agley.* (BURNS)

**airt** *noun* a direction or point of the compass: *The centre attracts visitors from a' the airts.*

**ashet** *noun* a large plate or shallow dish for cooking or serving food: *I'd rather have an ashet pie than a Scotch pie.* [French **assiette** plate]

**awfy** or **awfu** *adjective, adverb* awful or very: *They've made an awfy mess; She's awfy clever, that lassie.*

**baffies** *plural noun* slippers: *She's no away doon the shops wi they auld baffies on!*

**baggie** *or* **baggie minnie** *noun* a minnow, especially a large one: *When I was wee we used tae bring hame baggies in a jeely-jaur.*

**bahookie** *or* **behouchie** (*pronounced* ba-**hoo**-kee) a jocular word for a person's backside: *Is this carry-on no a pain in the bahookie?*

**bairn** *noun* **1** a baby or young child. This is used in most parts of the country, except primarily West Central Scotland, where **wean** tends to be used instead: *The wife's expecting a bairn; The bairns came home from the school.* **2** a nickname for a person from Falkirk [sense 2 springs from Falkirk's town motto: 'Better meddle wi the deil than the bairns o' Falkirk']

2

**ballop** (*pronounced* **bal**-op) *noun spoken in Galloway* the fly on a pair of trousers: *I suppose we'd better tell him his ballop's open.*

**barkit** (*pronounced* **bark**-it) *adjective spoken in Northeast* very dirty, especially encrusted with dried-on dirt: *Dinna put yer barkit boots on that chair!*

**barrie** *or* **barry** *adjective spoken in Edinburgh & Southeast* good or attractive: *Your hair looks really barrie like that.* [Romany]

**bashit** (*pronounced* **bash**-it) *adjective* mashed: *bashit neeps*

**bauchle** (*pronounced* **bawCH**-l) *or* **bachle** (*pronounced* **baCH**-l) *noun* literally a shabby or worn-out shoe, but

3

mostly used to mean an ungainly or shabby-looking person, especially a small one: *He's a right wee bauchle.*

**beastie** *noun* a small animal, particularly an insect, spider, or similar creepy-crawly: *What's that beastie on the curtain?*

**ben** *noun* a mountain, often part of the mountain's name, such as Ben Nevis or Ben Lomond: *You could see all the nearby bens from the top of the hill.* | *preposition, adverb* in, within, or into the inner or main part of a house: *Come ben the hoose; She was ben the kitchen making tea.* [Gaelic]

**bidie-in** (*pronounced* bide-ee-**in**) *noun* somebody who lives with another person as their husband or wife although they are not married: *Katia Labeque, McLaughlin's bidie-in and sometime musical partner*

> This is a nicely informal way of describing such a relationship; much couthier than 'live-in lover' or 'fellow householder'.

**bing** *noun* a large hill-like mound of waste from a mine or quarry: *Large oil-shale bings disfigured the countryside.*

**birk** *noun* a birch tree: *the birks o' Aberfeldy*

**birl** *verb* to spin or revolve: *Ma heid's birlin wi aw this noise.*

**black-affrontit** (*pronounced* blak-a-**frunt**-it) *or* **black-affronted** *adjective* very embarrassed or offended: *He was black-affrontit when she told him his ballop was open.*

**blaeberry** (*pronounced* **blay**-ber-i) *noun* an edible purplish-black berry, also known as a bilberry or whortleberry: *They're away picking blaeberries.*

**blaes** (*pronounced* **blayz**) *noun* crushed hardened clay or shale, reddish or bluish-grey in colour, which is used to form the top layer of a sports ground: *a blaes pitch*

> Blaes is rather less fun to play on than grass – and definitely not for those unwilling to suffer a skint knee!

**blaud** (*pronounced* **blahd**) *verb spoken in Northeast* to spoil or damage: *a park o' blaudit neeps*

**bleezin** *or* **bleezin fou** *adjective spoken in Northeast* very drunk: *He wis fair bleezin.*

**bodach** (*pronounced* **boe**-daCH) *noun spoken in North & West* an old man: *Ask the bodach if he's wanting a dram.* [Gaelic]

**boggin** *adjective* very dirty: *Dinnae sit on the good chair in thae boggin troosers!*

**boorach** *or* **bourach** (*pronounced* **boo**-raCH) *noun* 1 *spoken in Northeast* a group of assorted people or things: *a boorach o' fowk* 2 *spoken in Highlands* a mess or a disorderly state or heap: *I've*

only been away a week and the house is a
boorach. [Gaelic]

**bosie** (*pronounced* **boe**-zi) *noun spoken
in Northeast* **1** an embrace or cuddle:
*Gie's a bosie.* **2** the bosom: *Stick that
flooer in yer bosie.*

**bowff** *or* **bouff** (*pronounced* **bowf**)
*verb* **1** to smell strongly and
unpleasantly, like something rotten:
*Eeugh! This beer's bowffin!* **2** to bark, or
to speak or cough in a way that sounds
like a dog barking: *Who's dug is yon
that's aye bowffin?* | *noun* a strong
unpleasant smell: *The bowff in that
bedroom would sicken ye.*

**brae** (*pronounced* **bray**) *noun* a hill or
hillside: *Set a stout hert tae a stey brae.*

**braw** *adjective* fine or excellent: *It's a braw day.* [a Scots form of ***brave***]

**breeks** *plural noun* trousers or, occasionally, underpants: *Ma breeks're fallin doon!* [a Scots form of ***breeches***]

**breenge** *verb* to go somewhere or do something in a hasty and forceful, usually clumsy, way: *He breenged his way through the crowd.* | *noun* a forceful but clumsy rush: *There'll be quite a breenge when these doors open.*

**bubbly jock** *noun* a male turkey [probably because of the noise it makes]

**bumbaleerie** (*pronounced* bum-buh-**lee**-ree) *noun* the backside: *Ach, sit on yer bumbaleerie!*

9

### Who knew that was Scots?

Sometimes people come to Scotland expecting everyone to speak exclusively in broad Scots, rolling their r's as if their lives depended on it and havering on about 'a braw bricht moonlicht nicht'. Many Scots do have distinctive accents, and there are many local variations in both pronunciation and vocabulary. However, there are plenty of Scottish natives who don't speak broad Scots – indeed it used to be said that well-educated citizens of Inverness spoke the clearest form of English in Britain! – but many of them might be surprised to learn that when they think they are speaking standard English their vocabulary may be peppered with Scotticisms that would puzzle an English speaker from elsewhere. Take, for example, the following sentence, which might conceivably be spoken by a Scot: *If we can't uplift the brambles outwith office hours, I doubt they'll spoil.*

This doesn't fit in with the general idea of broad Scots, and yet there are several words here that could confuse an English person, who, attempting to convey the same meaning, would be more likely to say: *If we can't pick up the blackberries outside office hours, I believe they'll spoil.*

Similarly, a Scot being inoculated will have a jag, not a jab; go for the messages, not do the shopping; eat jeely pieces, not jam sandwiches; and wait for a bus or taxi at a stance, not a stand.

**bumfle** *noun* a wrinkle, crease, or fold in something: *Wait till I press the bumfles oot that shirt.* | *verb* to put wrinkles or creases in something: *My skirt had got all bumfled up at the back.* [from earlier Scots **bumph** meaning a lump or bump]

**burn** *noun* a stream or brook: *Is there fish in that burn?*

**burny** *adjective* extremely hot: *Use a cloth tae hold that dish; it's burny.*

**buroo** (*pronounced* buh-**roo** *or* **broo**) *or* **broo** *noun* the dole, or the office where people sign on for their dole money: *Has your buroo money come through yet?*; *He's been on the broo for years.* [from Employment *Bureau*, a former name for a Jobcentre]

**but-and-ben** (*pronounced* but-and-**ben**) *noun* an old-fashioned rural cottage consisting of two rooms, usually a kitchen and living room: *They're renting out the but-and-ben as a holiday cottage.*

**buttery** *or* **buttery rowie** *noun spoken in Aberdeen* a type of crumbly, butter-rich, bread roll: *Two cups of coffee and a couple of butteries, please.*

**byke** *or* **bike** (*pronounced* **bike**) *noun* a wasps' nest: *We had a wasps' byke in the attic last autumn.*

**byordinar** (*pronounced* bie-**or**-di-nar) *adjective, adverb* unusual or exceptionally: *a maist byordinar day; It's byordinar cauld for May.* [from **by** in the sense beyond, plus ***ordinar*** ordinary]

**byre** (*pronounced* **bire**) *noun* a shed or stable where cows are kept: *The kye are in the byre.*

**cailleach** (*pronounced* **kayl**-yaCH *or* **kal**-yaCH) *noun spoken in North & West* an old woman: *My memory of her is of a vague chain-smoking cailleach in eccentric garb and heavy henna.* [Gaelic]

**caller** (*pronounced* **kal**-er) *adjective* fresh, especially referring to fish, fruit, or vegetables: *caller herring*

**camstairy** (*pronounced* kam-**stair**-ee) *or* **camsteerie** (*pronounced* kam-**stee**-ree) *adjective* quarrelsome, stubborn, or unruly: *Let the camstairy auld deil dae whit he likes.*

**cantrip** *noun* **1** a spell or magic charm:

*By some devilish cantrip slight, each in its cold hand held a light. (BURNS)* **2** a playful trick: *The bairns wouldnae be playin such cantrips if their faither was in the hoose.*

**carnaptious** (*pronounced* kar-**nap**-shuss) *adjective* grumpy, bad-tempered, or irritable: *She's a carnaptious auld biddy!* [from **knap** bite]

**caul** (*pronounced* **kawl**) *noun spoken in South* a weir or a dam: *A broken branch was stuck at the caul.*

**causey** (*pronounced* **kaw**-zi) *noun*
**1** a cobbled street, road, or way: *That causey's awful slippy when it's rainin.*
**2** a cobble or paving stone: *She's a lump on her heid the size o' a causey.*

15

**ceud míle fáilte** (*pronounced* **kee**-ut **mee**-luh **fah**-il-tya) *interjection* a hundred thousand welcomes: *He couldnae spell 'ceud míle fáilte' so he just wrote 'Hiya!'* [Gaelic]

> This greeting is often seen on place-name signs for towns, as if one, genuinely warm, welcome were not enough for anybody.

**champit tatties** *plural noun* mashed potatoes, one of the traditional accompaniments to haggis, along with bashit neeps, in a Burns Supper

**chauve** *or* **tyauve** (*pronounced* **chawv**) *spoken in Northeast verb* to struggle, strive, or work hard, often with little to show for one's exertions: *Still chauvin awa?* | *noun* a struggle: *It's a sair chauve for a half loaf.*

**chookie** *or* **chookie birdie** *noun* a bird: *Hear that wee chookie singin? That's a blackbird.*

**chuckie** *or* **chuckie stane** *noun* a stone or pebble of throwable size: *throwing chuckies in the water*

**clabber** *or* **glabber** *noun spoken in Southwest* mud, earth, or clay: *Ma trainers are still aw clabber fae T in the Park.* [Gaelic *clàbar* meaning mud or a puddle]

**clachan** (*pronounced* **klaCH**-an) *noun* a small village or hamlet: *He was born in a wee clachan in Argyll.* [Gaelic, meaning stone]

This word was originally used
only of Highland villages,
but its use is now more
widespread.

**clack** (*pronounced* **klak**) *or* **claick**
(*pronounced* **klayk**) *spoken in Northeast*
*noun* gossip or chat: *Never heed their*
*daft clack.* | *verb* to gossip or chat:
*How about some graftin, instead of*
*clackin away like a pair o' sweetiewives?*
[probably from one of its original
meanings: the clattering sound of a mill
in operation]

**claes** (*pronounced* **klayz**) *plural noun*
clothes: *Hing on till Ah get some claes*
*on.* The saying **back to auld claes and**
**porridge** means a return to normality
after a period of jollity, celebration, or

indulgence: *After Hogmanay it's back to auld claes and porridge for us.*

**clanjamfrie** (*pronounced* klan-**jam**-free) *or* **clamjamfrie** (*pronounced* klam-**jam**-free) *noun* **1** a group of people, usually used to dismiss them as a rabble: *There's naebody wi' any sense in the hale clanjamfrie!* **2** a varied assortment of things; a mixed bag: *the clamjamfrie of tenements, courtyards and closes which forms Edinburgh's Old Town*

**clapshot** *noun* a dish of boiled potatoes and turnips which have been mashed together in roughly equal quantities: *Lunch is fillets of cod served with clapshot, roasted peppers, and chilli oil.*

**cleg** *or* **clegg** *noun* a horse-fly with a painful bite: *Once ye've been but wi' a cleg, ye're no feart o' midgies.* [Old Norse *klegge*]

**clipshears** *or* **clipshear** *noun* an earwig: *There was hundreds of clipshears and slaters under the flowerpot when she lifted it.* [from the resemblance of the pincers at the tip of the creature's abdomen to shears]

**clishmaclaver** (*pronounced* klish-ma-**clay**-ver) *noun* gossip or incessant chatter: *Ye should be ashamed o' yersel, repeatin clishmaclaver like yon!* [a combination of two Scots words, **clish** to repeat gossip, and **claver** to talk idly]

**cloot** *noun* a piece of cloth or a cloth

used as a duster, etc: *Dicht roon the sink wi' a cloot.*

**clootie dumpling** (*pronounced* **kloo**-ti) *noun* a rich dark fruitcake served as a dessert, like a Christmas pudding. It is boiled or steamed in a **cloot** or cloth: *Ma grannie used tae pit a sixpenny bit in the clootie dumplin for some lucky soul tae find.*

**cludgie** (*pronounced* **kluj**-i) *noun spoken in Central* a toilet: *A wee boy's got locked in the cludgie.* [perhaps a mixture of *closet* and *ludge*, a Scots form of lodge]

**clype** *or* **clipe** *noun* a person who tells tales or informs on his or her friends, colleagues, or schoolmates: *Just you keep your mouth shut, ya wee clype!* | *verb* to

tell tales or inform on: *We'd have been
all right if she hadnae cliped on us tae the
heidie.* [related to Old English **cleopian** to
call or name]

**coggle** *verb* to wobble, rock, or be
unsteady: *Tiger Woods' ball coggled for a
minute on the lip of the eighteenth hole.*

**coggly** *adjective* shaky or unsteady: *Find
another table; this yin's a wee bit coggly.*

**collieshangie** (*pronounced* kol-ee-
**shang**-gee) *noun* a loud and disorderly
commotion or quarrel: *What's all this
collieshangie out in the street?* [the word
used to mean a dogfight, so perhaps it
comes from **collie** the breed of dog and
**shangie** a chain or leash connecting two
dogs]

**connach** (*pronounced* **kon**-naCH) *verb spoken in Northeast* **1** to spoil, in various different ways: *The crop was clean connached by the weather; He connacht the fairm wi his drinkin; The thunder connacht the milk; It wis his mither at aye connacht him.* **2** to tire out: *The wee lad wis fair connached wi the lang walk.* [perhaps from the old Gaelic **conach**, meaning a disease of cattle]

**coorie** *or* **courie** *verb* to nestle or snuggle: *He cooried in to his mother's side.* [from the Scots **coor** meaning cower]

**corbie** *noun* a crow: *twa corbies sittin on a wa'* [from Old French **corbin**]

**The earliest Scots**

The origins of the Scottish people are complicated, and Scotland's history involves much conquest and reconquest by various peoples. However, two particular tribes have strong claims to being in at the start of the Scottish nation: the Picts and the Scots.

The Picts were a fairly mysterious set of people. Records of their language exist on a few beautifully carved stones in the north of Scotland but these inscriptions remain largely undeciphered. We know that places with names beginning 'Pit-' were probably Pictish settlements but that's about it. We don't even know what they called themselves; the label 'Picts' comes from Latin *Picti*, meaning painted men, suggesting that they were heavily tattooed or painted themselves with woad. They were said to be a relatively small, dark-haired people. Apparently they gave any Romans who ventured north of Hadrian's Wall such a hard time that 'haste ye back' fell on deaf ears. They were converted to Christianity in the sixth century by Saint Columba and other intrepid missionaries, and their kingdom came to be known as Alba, a name which endures as the Gaelic name for Scotland.

We know more about the Scots, the Gaelic-speaking tribes from Ireland who started raiding what is now Argyll in the fifth and sixth centuries before deciding that they liked it so much that they preferred to stay. They established the kingdom of Dalriada, which took in much of Northern Ireland, the Western Isles and the western mainland. The Scots gradually conquered the Pictish lands, absorbing or killing off the Picts themselves, until their ninth-century king Kenneth MacAlpine was able to rule as Kenneth I of Scotland. Nowadays you don't have to be a Gael to be a Scot; you just have to arrange to be born here.

**corrie-fisted** *adjective* left-handed: *The teacher used tae gie us the belt if we were corrie-fisted.* [from the Gaelic **cearr** left or wrong hand]

> If your surname is Kerr or Carr, it's likely that you had a left-handed ancestor in the distant past.

**corrie-fister** *noun* a left-handed person

**coup** or **cowp** (*pronounced* **kowp**) *noun* **1** a rubbish tip: *He's away tae the coup wi' his auld computer.* **2** a dirty or untidy place: *Tidy up that coup of a room of yours.* | *verb* to turn or fall over: *The wean couped her bowl onto the floor.* [from the Middle English **cowp** to strike]

**couthy** *or* **couthie** (*pronounced*
**kooth**-i) *adjective* **1** plain, homely, or
unsophisticated: *His poetry unaffectedly*
*blended the couthy with the cosmopolitan.*
**2** comfortable and snug: *They gave us*
*a braw, couthy wee room on the ground*
*floor.* **3** sociable and friendly: *They're*
*such a couthy bunch that you'll soon make*
*friends.* [from the Old English *cūth*
known]

**cowk** *verb* *spoken in Northeast* to retch
or vomit: *The sea got rough and ane or*
*twa bairns were cowkin ower the side.*

**crabbit** (*pronounced* **krab**-it) *adjective*
grumpy or bad-tempered: *He's aye*
*crabbit first thing in the morning.* [a Scots
form of ***crabbed***]

**crannie** *noun spoken in Northeast* the little finger, or pinkie: *the size o' your crannie*

**craw steps** *or* **corbie steps** *plural noun* the small steps on the gable of a roof in traditional Scottish architecture: *We could make out the steeples and craw steps of the old town.*

**creel** *noun* a large basket used to carry bread or fish: *plenty herring to fill the creel* A *labster creel* is a wickerwork trap for catching lobsters and shellfish: *The fisherman told us that there was a labster creel on the seabed under each of the little buoys.*

**creeshie** *adjective* greasy or dirty: *Ah'm no eatin ony mair of thae creeshie* *burgers o' theirs.* [from **creesh** fat or tallow]

**crivvens** *or* **criffens** *interjection* an exclamation of surprise: *Crivvens, is that the time already?*

> This word is considered so inoffensive as to be quite suitable for ministers and aunties, even though some people think it was originally a form of **Christ defend us.**

**crowdie** (*pronounced* **krow**-di) *noun* a soft white cheese made by straining the whey from soured milk and beating up the remaining curd with salt: *The teashop served home-made scones with bramble* *jam amd crowdie.* [perhaps from **crud**, an earlier form of **curd**]

> It might be best to keep this rather unfortunate association with 'crud' at the back of your mind the next time you see crowdie on the menu.

**cuddy** *or* **cuddie** *noun* a donkey or a horse: *My legs are as stiff as an auld cuddy.* [possibly a nickname for **Cuthbert**, although that seems rather a high-falutin name for a donkey]

**cundy** *noun* the gutter at the side of the road or the cover of a drain: *The cundy was choked with dead leaves and rubbish.* [a Scottish pronunciation of the English **conduit**]

**cushie-doo** (*pronounced* koosh-ee-**doo**) *or* **cushat-doo** (*pronounced* koosh-at-**doo**) *or* **cushie** *noun* a wood pigeon: *Ah hear a cushie-doo cooin in yon tree, but Ah cannae spot it.* [from the English **cushat** plus *doo*, a Scots word for pigeon]

**dachle** (*pronounced* **daCH**-l) *verb* spoken in Northeast to dawdle or loiter: *Dinnae dachle on the road or it'll be dark afore ye get back.*

**daffin** *noun* playful or foolish behaviour: *He wis aye wan for daffin wi' the lassies.*

**dander** *or* **dauner** (*pronounced* **dawn**-er) *noun* a stroll: *I'm just away for a wee dander.* | *verb* to stroll: *You can dander across the Solway sands to Rough*

*Island, but beware of being stranded by the incoming tide.*

**darg** *noun* a day's work or a task to be done: *He'll never ken the satisfaction o' finishin a good day's darg.* [from a contraction of **day-work**]

**daud** (*pronounced* **dawd**) *or* **dad** *noun* a lump or chunk of something: *Gie's a daud o' breid tae keep me goin.*

**deave** (*pronounced* **deev**) *verb* to deafen someone, or to bewilder or weary them with noise or talk: *Grandad was always deaving us with his war stories.*

**deek** *spoken in Edinburgh & Southeast verb* to look at or see something: *Deek this gadgie.* | *noun* a look at something: *Have a deek out the window.* [Romany]

**deif** (*pronounced* **deef**) *adjective* deaf:
*I'm talking to you! Are ye deif or*
*something?*

**deil** (*pronounced* **deel**) *noun* the devil:
*They say the deil looks after his ain.*

**dicht** (*pronounced* **diCHt** *or* **dite**) *verb*
to wipe something clean: *Dicht roon the*
*sink.* | *noun* a wipe: *Gie your face a dicht.*
[Old English *diht* to arrange]

**diddy** *noun* **1** a female breast or nipple:
*a photie o' a lassie showin her diddies*
**2** *spoken in Glasgow area* a foolish
person: *D'ye know nothin, ya wee diddy?*

**dirl** *verb* to vibrate or shake: *The noise*
*of the bagpipes made the very rafters*
*dirl.*

### Gaelic voices

Nowadays we tend to think of Gaelic as being spoken only in the Highlands and Islands, but in fact it was once the everyday language of most of what is now Scotland. Indeed it was commonly spoken in the southwest of the country until the sixteenth century. The ancient language is now undergoing something of a revival in Lowland cities, especially in the Glasgow area, where Gaelic-medium schools have been established.

Its influence on Scots is most immediately apparent in place names, where words like *ben*, *glen*, and *loch* have come straight from Gaelic, and in surnames, with the ubiquitous prefix *Mac-*. Things that were originally connected with Gaelic culture have often retained their Gaelic names, as in the case of *clan*, *claymore*, *sporran*, *quaich*, *sgian-dhu*, and *pibroch*. Gaelic words also crop up in the otherwise Scots speech of inhabitants of the north and west, as in *bourach* and *cailleach*, and Scottish people all over the world are used to toasting one another with the Gaelic phrase *slainte mhath*, especially when drinking whisky (from the Gaelic *uisge*), perhaps at a *ceilidh*.

Many Gaelic terms have made the transition (via Scots) to standard English itself, including *galore*, *gob*, and *slogan*. Kilt-wearing Gaels in the Lowlands were once commonly taunted by phrases such as 'Donald, where's yer troosers?' It is perhaps ironic that without the Gaelic word *triubhas* (which entered Scots as *trews*) the English-language term for this indispensable garment would have had to be something else altogether.

**disjaskit** (*pronounced* dis-**jas**-kit)
*adjective* miserable and unhappy, often
being completely exhausted or worn
out into the bargain: *He was in a maist
disjaskit state.* [probably a variant of
*dejected*]

**doakie** (*pronounced* **doe**-ki) *noun* a
person's backside: *She gave the bairn a
skelp on the doakie.*

**docken** (*pronounced* **dok**-en *or* **doe**-
ken) *noun* **1** the dock plant or any of
its leaves: *Rub that nettle-sting with
a docken.* **2** a thing of no value or
importance: *It's no worth a docken.*

**doitit** (*pronounced* **doyt**-it) *adjective*
foolish or childish, often applied to older
people suggesting that they are senile:

*Ah've lost ma bus pass, doitit aul deil that Ah am!* [probably related to the English *dotage*]

**donnert** (*pronounced* **don**-nert) *adjective* stupid or stunned: *She was that donnert wi' the news she had tae sit doon.*

**doo** *noun* a dove, or even a lowly pigeon: *The weans were feedin the doos in George Square.*

**dook** *or* **douk** *verb* to duck, dip, or bathe: *a bonny white swan, dookin its heid intae the watter* | *noun* an act of ducking, dipping, or bathing: *Who's for a dook in the loch?*

**doolie** *noun* a foolish person: *Ye forgot tae stir the paint, ya doolie!*

37

**doon-bye** *adverb* down there, that is, in a place that has already been mentioned: *"Is it near Dumfries he stays?" "Aye, he lives doon-bye."*

**dottled** *adjective spoken in Northeast* confused, muddled or senile: *I may be old, but I'm no dottled yet.* [related to the English *dotage*]

**doup** (*pronounced* **dowp**) *noun* a person's buttocks: *Ye'll get a boot in yer doup if yer nae careful!* [Dutch *dop* a shell]

**dowt** *noun* a cigarette-end: *Some eejit flung a dowt intae the bushes and startit a fire.* [English dialect, meaning to put out a fire]

**drappie** *noun* a little drop, especially

of spirits: *Then we had a drappie, just to make us happy.*

**dree one's weird** *phrase* to endure the fate that destiny has decreed for you: *Aye, it's hard luck on the lassie, but she'll just have to dree her weird like the rest of us.* [the main elements of this are essentially old English words: *dree* meaning to suffer, and **weird** meaning fate]

**dreich** (*pronounced* **dreeCH**) *adjective* **1** dreary or tedious: *It's one of the dreichest stretches of road in all Scotland.* **2** referring to weather, wet or dismal: *It's awful dreich this morning.*

Anyone who spends a winter in Scotland will soon be

able to identify weather
that qualifies as dreich, and
understand how fitting a
term it is!

**drookit** *or* **droukit** (*pronounced*
**drook**-it) *adjective* drenched or soaked:
*The wee soul got caught in that rain and
came in drookit.*

**drooth** *or* **drouth** *noun* a thirst: *You've
got some drooth on ye the night!* [a Scots
form of ***drought***]

**dwam** *or* **dwaum** *noun* someone
who is ***in a dwam*** is in a stupor or a
daydream: *Sorry, I didn't catch what
you said. I was away in a wee dwam.*
[Germanic]

**dwine** *verb* to decline in health or

vigour; to waste away: *At the rate she's dwining, the auld soul's not long for this world.* | *noun* a decline in health or vigour: *He went into a dwine and died the next day.*

**eejit** (*pronounced* **ee**-jit) *noun* an idiot: *There ought to be stronger measures taken to ban such eejits from being anywhere near guns.*

**een** *plural noun* eyes: *Ah havenae shut ma een a' nicht.* (One eye is an *ee*)

**erse** (*pronounced* **erss**) *noun* a person's backside: *Shift yer erse, wee man!*

**ettle** (*pronounced* **et**-l) *verb* to attempt to do something: *ettlin tae scrieve in Doric* [Old Norse]

## More than a game

It was a Scotsman, Bill Shankly, who said that while some people talked about football as though it were a matter of life and death, the game was in fact much more important than that. Many of his countrymen would concur with that view. Although rugby has its area of influence in Edinburgh and the Borders, and the Gaelic sport of shinty has its own heartland in the Highlands, football is the only team sport that inspires mass interest in Scotland.

Domestic football is dominated by the 'old firm' of Celtic and Rangers. These teams enjoy a bitter rivalry, exacerbated by the fact that Celtic's support is largely of Catholic and Irish background, while Rangers fans are associated with Protestant Unionism. Matches between the two excite high emotions and grudges are nursed for decades.

Scottish football reached a high water mark in 1967, when Celtic's 'Lisbon Lions' won the European Cup. In the same year, Scotland's national side won a famous victory over the English, thus mitigating the grief felt at the auld enemy's World Cup triumph of the previous year and prompting a widespread belief that it was actually Scotland who were the real world champions.

Perhaps this success raised expectation among Scottish fans to unrealistic levels, for subsequent years have brought mainly disappointment. This was typified by the failure of Ally McLeod's much-heralded side in the 1978 World Cup and ignominious defeat at the hands of Costa Rica in 1990.

With Scotland no longer assured of glory on the field, the country's supporters have made the best of the situation, dressing flamboyantly, rooting for any team that happens to be playing England, and taking pride in their reputation for being the friendliest and most passionate fans in the world.

**fae** (*pronounced* **fay**) *or* **frae** (*pronounced* **fray**) *preposition* from: *some guy fae Tollcross; Where'd he get that fae?*

> The east of Scotland punk band The Rezillos had a singer who called herself Fay Fife, thus economically allowing her name and place of origin to be identified simultaneously.

**fankle** *verb* to tangle something: *The fishing line had got all fankled up.* | *noun* a tangle or a state of confusion: *Don't get yourself in a fankle.*

**fantoosh** (*pronounced* fan-**toosh**) *adjective* ostentatious or pretentious: *Some of their outfits were awfy fantoosh.*

[perhaps from the French *fantoche* a puppet]

**farl** *noun* a three-sided oatcake or piece of shortbread made by quartering a large round one: *The kind of scones I like best are soda farls.* [from the older *fardel* meaning a fourth part]

**fash** *verb* to trouble, bother, or annoy: *Dinna fash yersel.* [Old French]

**faughie** (*pronounced* **fawCH**-ee) *adjective* spoken in North pale and sickly-looking: *I thought she was lookin a wee bit faughie.*

**faur** (*pronounced* **for**) *adjective, adverb* far: *Ye're faur better gaun the Stirling road.*

**feart** (*pronounced* **feert**) *adjective* afraid: *Away hame if ye're feart.*

**feartie** (*pronounced* **feer**-tee) *noun*
a coward: *He wouldnae go on the
roller-coaster. He's a right big feartie,
isn't he?*

**ferntickle** (*pronounced* **fern**-tik-l) *or*
**fernietickle** (*pronounced* **fern**-ee-tik-l)
*noun* a freckle: *Aw, the wean's cute
wee face is covered in fernietickles!*
[from the old belief that freckles were
the result of being touched or tickled
by a fern]

**ficher** (*pronounced* **fiCH**-er) *verb
spoken in Northeast* to fumble or fiddle
with something: *There's nae point in
ficherin aboot wi' it.*

**ficherie** (*pronounced* **fiCH**-er-ree)
*adjective spoken in Northeast* awkward,

fiddly or bothersome: *That's ower ficherie a job for me.*

**fiddler's biddin'** *noun* a last-minute invitation to some social occasion, such as might be issued to a violin player who will provide the entertainment: *She said she was too proud to go to the wedding on such a fiddler's biddin'.*

**finnan haddie** *or* **haddock** *noun* a smoked haddock: *It's years since I had a finnan haddie for my breakfast.* [from a local pronunciation of **Findon**, a village south of Aberdeen]

**fit** *noun* a foot: *The line was nine fit lang.* The saying *a gaun fit's aye gettin* means the active and industrious are the ones who will make the most profit or progress | *pronoun spoken in Northeast & North* what: *Ye ken fine fit Ah mean.*

> This is an example of the Northeast tendency to pronounce the 'wh-' sound as 'f-'. In this way the question *fit like?* means 'how are you?'

**fitba** (*pronounced* **fit**-baw) *noun spoken in Glasgow area* football: *Ye cannae call that big numpty a fitba player.*

> Other regions have their own dialect forms of the word, such as *fittie* and *futtie*

**fleg** *verb* to frighten: *Dinna fleg the bairns wi' yer daft stories.* | *noun* a fright or scare: *Ah got such a fleg when the doorbell went!*

**fley** (*pronounced* **flay**) *verb* to frighten or scare: *I'll soon fley the likes o' them awa'.*

**flype** *verb* to turn something inside out: *She sat by the fire flyping socks and darning them.*

**flyte** *verb* to scold or complain bitterly at someone: *It's no use flyting at one another.* | *noun* (also ***flyting***) a dispute or argument: *Whit's a' the flyte aboot?*

> Historically, ***flyting*** was a competition between two poets to decide which could write the most wittily abusive verse about the other.

**foo** *adverb* *spoken in Northeast* how: *Foo are ye daein'?*

49

**footer** or **fouter** *verb* to potter or fiddle: *She's footering about in the garden I think.* | *noun* **1** a person who footers: *Will ye leave that phone alone, ye wee footer!* **2** an awkward or fiddly task: *It's a bit of a footer to get those wee screws back in.*

**footery** or **fouterie** *adjective* awkward or fiddly: *Ah havenae the patience for footery wee jobs like that.*

**forby** or **forbye** (*pronounced* for-**bie**) *preposition, adverb* **1** besides or in addition: *There's enough for everybody and more forby.* **2** except: *The whole lot's here, forby one or two.*

**forfochen** (*pronounced* for-**foCH**-en) or **forfochtin** (*pronounced* for-**foCH**-tin) *adjective* exhausted or worn out: *By the end of the open day we were fair forfochen and glad to get home.*

**forkietail** *noun* an earwig (sometimes shortened to *forkie*): *She found a wee forkietail underneath the sheets in the press.*

**fornenst** (*pronounced* for-**nenst**) *preposition* situated against or in front of something: *The hoose sat richt fornenst the burn.*

**fou** *or* **fu'** (*pronounced* **foo**) *adjective* **1** full: *He never halted till the bunker was fou o' coal.* **2** drunk: *Dinnae serve him ony mair, he's fou.*

**Furry Boots City** *noun* a nickname for the city of Aberdeen: *We've had a request* *for Andy Stewart from a listener up in Furry Boots City.*

One of the distinctive dialect features in the Aberdeen area is pronouncing the 'wh-' sound as 'f-'. In this way, someone asked by an Aberdonian 'Whereabouts do you come from?' would hear something like 'fauraeboots …'. The fact that the area is not known for balmy temperatures also helps.

**fykie** (*pronounced* **fie**-ki) *adjective* involving a lot of delicate or intricate work: *a fykie task*

**gads** *interjection* a mild expression of
disgust or dismay: *Gads! Would that no
sicken ye?* [a euphemistic form of **God**]

**gallus** (*pronounced* **gal**-luss) *adjective*
**1** self-confident, daring, and often
slightly cheeky or reckless: *He's too gallus
to be intimidated by anyone.* **2** *spoken
in Glasgow* stylish or impressive: *Have
you seen Davie's new guitar? It's gallus!*
[originally a disapproving term, meaning
wild, rascally, and deserving to be
hanged from a *gallows*]

**galshachs** (*pronounced* **gal**-shaCHs)
*plural noun spoken in Northeast* sweets,
cakes, sweet biscuits, and other sweet
but not necessarily healthy delicacies:
*empire biscuits, cream buns, an suchlike
galshachs* [perhaps related to the Scots

53

*gulsoch* jaundice or any sickness caused by over-eating]

**gang** *verb* to go: *The best laid schemes o' mice and men gang aft agley.* (Burns)

> This is now rather old-fashioned or literary, but still recognized by most people through being very common in folk songs and poems.

**gawkie** (*pronounced* **gaw**-kee) *noun* a person who looks stupid, clumsy, or awkward: *Who's yon gawkie clackin wi' yer wee sister?*

**gawkit** (*pronounced* **gaw**-kit) *adjective* stupid, clumsy, or awkward-looking: *a gawkit teenager*

**gean** (*pronounced* **geen**) *noun* a wild cherry tree or its fruit: *a' thae roses an geans will turn tae bloom* [Old French *guigne*]

**geet** (*pronounced* **geet**) *noun spoken in Northeast* a child, especially an obnoxious or illegitimate one: *a hoor's geet* [a local variant of *get* and *git*]

**geggie** (*pronounced* **geg**-ee) *noun spoken in Glasgow area* **1** the mouth, most often heard in the command: *Shut your geggie!* **2** a child's homemade vehicle constructed from pram wheels, wooden boxes, etc: *fleein doon the brae in a geggie*

> It is now very rare to see a child with a home-made

vehicle, in these days of skateboards and trainers with wheels in the heel, but the word will still be found in nostalgic contexts.

**gey** (*pronounced* **gie** *or* **gay**) *adverb* very or exceptionally: *gey few; It's gey warm in here.*

**gillie** *or* **ghillie** (*pronounced* **gil-ee**) *noun* a person employed to act as a guide and assistant to people who are out angling or shooting: *Her father worked as a gillie on an estate in Perthshire.* [Gaelic *gille* a lad or servant]

**gimmer** *noun* a young ewe between its first and second shearing: *He'd a substantial number of lambs, gimmers,* *and ewes.* [Old Norse **gymbr** a female lamb]

**ging** *verb spoken in Northeast* to go: *They're just a pack o' sheep, wi'oot the guts to ging aff on their own.*

**girn** *verb* to moan, complain, or grumble: *The losers were still girning and whining about the alleged injustice they had suffered.*

**glaikit** *or* **glaiket** (*pronounced* **glay**-kit) *adjective* silly, foolish, or thoughtless: *Go and get the mop, you glaikit lump!*; *That's a glaikit way of doing it.*

**glaur** (*pronounced* **glowr**) *noun* soft, sticky mud: *We were up to our ankles in glaur.*

### The call of the pipes

Bagpipes are not unique to Scotland – versions of the instrument are known in many cultures from Northumberland to Nepal – but the Highland bagpipe has come to be one of the identifying icons of Scottish culture as it is perceived by the wider world. Not everyone in Scotland loves the bagpipes; for every one who feels his or her heart lifted by the skirl of the pipes as a kilted band marches past, there will be others who reach for the earplugs or fantasize about sticking a big pin into the wretched bag. Not even an aficionado of pibroch would necessarily relish living next-door to someone learning to play. Yet the instrument continues to be popular, whether at the level of the busker in Edinburgh's Princes Street or the highly trained exponent of the intricacies of *ceol mor* (the big music) at piping festivals.

The pipes have always had a connection with martial matters. In earlier times Highland clans would be led into battle by a piper playing familiar stirring tunes, and this tradition is continued to this day in Scots regiments. Indeed, when the British government banned Highland dress in the aftermath of the Jacobite Rebellion, the bagpipes were also proscribed as 'an instrument of war'. Thousands of Gaels, denied the use of the instrument for peaceful purposes such as accompanying Highland dance, had to improvise with *port a beul* (mouth music) in which someone would 'sing' the tunes that would normally be played on the pipes.

Playing the pipes is thirsty work and it is a long-established proverb that a piper's 'drooth' is the hardest to slake.

**golach** (*pronounced* **gol**-aCH) *noun*
*spoken in East* a beetle: *A muckle great*
*golach came crawlin oot frae under the*
*stane.* [from the Gaelic ***gobhlag*** an
earwig or forked object]

**goonie** *noun* a nightie or other kind
of gown, such as one worn by a patient
going to the operating theatre in
hospital: *Ah hate these goonies they gie*
*ye in hospital that cannae close up the*
*back.*

**gowan** (*pronounced* **gow**-an) *noun* a
daisy or, occasionally, another similar
white or yellow flower: *We twa hae run*
*about the braes, And pou'd the gowans*
*fine.* (BURNS)

**gowf** (*pronounced* **gowf**) *noun* golf:

*The match will take place at Loudoun Gowf Club in Galston.*

> This is slightly old-fashioned, but people still use the word jocularly and it appears in the official name of some golf clubs.

**gowfer** *noun* a golfer: *A mad keen gowfer will play in any weather.*

**gowk** (*pronounced* **gowk**) *noun* **1** a cuckoo: *a gowk's nest* **2** a fool or simpleton: *What are you waiting for, you daft gowk?* [Old Norse *gaukr*]

> In some parts of Eastern Scotland, the victim of an April Fool's Day trick is known as an **April gowk.**

**graith** (*pronounced* **greth**) *noun* equipment, tools, or gear needed for a task: *fishing graith; Hurry up and get the graith into the van.*

**gravit** (*pronounced* **grah**-vit *or* **graw**-vit) *noun* *spoken in Northeast* a scarf, especially a warm woollen one: *He had a big red gravit roon his thrapple.* [from *cravat*]

**greet** *verb* to cry or weep: *What's the wean greetin for?* (The past tense is *grat* and the past participle is *grutten*) | *noun* a period of time spent crying: *I like a good greet at the pictures now and again.* **Greetin face** is a name often applied to someone who always looks miserable: *I see Greetin face was moaning about the referee again.* A **Greetin Teenie** is a person who is always complaining: *Nothing's good enough for the old Greetin Teenie.*

**grippie** *adjective spoken in Northeast* mean or miserly: *Dinnae expect a tip frae yon grippie auld deil.*

> Northeast Scotland is popularly regarded as having more than its fair share of skinflints, and so it is not surprising that its vocabulary should be well stocked with words such as this.

**grosset** *noun* a gooseberry: *My grannie used to make grosset wine and bramble jelly.* [from French **groseille**]

**grue** (*pronounced* **groo**) *verb* to shudder or shiver from fear or disgust: *The taste*

63

*of that medicine would make ye grue.*
Something which **gars ye grue** is so
frightening or horrific that it makes your
blood run cold

**guddle** *noun* an untidy or messy place
or state: *He's left all my papers in a right
guddle.* | *verb* to try to catch a fish from a
river or pond with your bare hands: *Two
boys were lying on the bank with their hands
in the water, obviously guddling for trout.*

**gushet** (*pronounced* **gush**-it) *noun* a
triangular piece of land, such as one
between two roads which meet at a
sharp angle: *There's a bus stop at the
gushet over there.*

**gutties** *plural noun spoken in West
Central & Southwest* plimsolls or

trainers: *The boy's needin a new pair o' gutties for gym.* [from **gutta-percha**, a type of rubber used to make soles]

**gweed** *spoken in Northeast adjective* good: *She gied the press ablow the sink a gweed redd up.* | *noun* a euphemism for God: *Gweed kens fa did it.*

**gype** (*pronounced* **gipe**) *noun spoken in Northeast* a foolish or stupid person: *He's a glaikit gype.*

**haaf** (*pronounced* **haf**) *noun spoken in Orkney & Shetland* the open sea, as distinct from coastal waters: *haaf fishing*

**haar** (*pronounced* **har**) *noun* a cold mist or fog from the North Sea which frequently occurs along the East coast: *The east-coast haar has lowered* *temperatures in Edinburgh in the morning and evening recently.* [Dutch]

**habble** *noun* **1** a clumsy, not particularly successful, attempt to do something: *He was having a habble trying to get the childproof lid off the bottle.* **2** a mess: *You've made a right habble of that bedroom.*

**hackit** or **hacket** (*pronounced* **hak-**it) *adjective* ugly, definitely not good-looking: *I do not fancy her. She's hackit!*

**haddie** *noun* **1** a haddock: *a braw haddie for my tea* **2** a clumsy or silly person: *The car's steering is so good that you have to be a real haddie to get it to misbehave.*

**haet** (*pronounced* **hayt**) *noun* the smallest amount possible, a whit or iota:

*not a haet of difference* [a shortening of
the phrase **deil hae it** devil have it]

**hain** (*pronounced* **hayn**) *verb spoken in
Northeast* to save something for possible
future use: *He's haint aa the pokes he got
fae the supermairket.* [from Old Norse
**hegna** to hedge or protect]

**hallirackit** (*pronounced* hal-lee-**rak**-
it) *adjective spoken in Northeast* wild,
rowdy and irresponsible: *She's a damned
hallirackit bitch.* [from Old Scots **halok** a
silly thoughtless girl]

**hamefare** (*pronounced* **haym**-fair)
*noun spoken in Orkney & Shetland* the
occasion of a newly married woman
moving into her new house and the
subsequent party celebrating this:

*Martha's hamefare became so famous that a song was written about it.*

**hap** *verb* to cover or wrap: *distant hills happed in mist* To **hap up** means to wrap up or dress warmly for cold weather: *well happed up against the cold* | *noun* a protective covering, such as a heavy coat: *That's a good warm hap you've got there.*

**harl** *verb* to cover the outside walls of a building with a mixture of lime and gravel or small stones; to roughcast them: *a small development of harled council houses* | *noun* the mixture of lime and gravel used in covering walls in this way: *the white Skye marble which, ground into chips, provided the harl finish to houses in the north*

**haud** (*pronounced* **hawd**) *verb* to hold: *Haud on and Ah'll chum you up the road.* (The past participle is **hudden** or **hauden**) | *noun* a hold: *Wait till Ah get a haud o' him.*

**hauf** (*pronounced* **hawf**) *adjective* half: *a hauf-loaf* | *noun* a small glass of whisky. Originally this was a measure of half a gill, and a **wee hauf** was a quarter-gill, but both terms are now used more loosely to mean any smallish measure: *There's a guy having a fly hauf in the toilets.* A **hauf an a hauf** is a whisky served with a half-pint of beer as a chaser

**haver** *or* **haiver** (*pronounced* **hay-**ver) *verb* to talk nonsense: *What's he havering about?* | *noun* **havers** is nonsense: *Don't give me your havers!*

69

## Places with strange-sounding names

Visitors to Scotland may often have difficulty in pronouncing the place names they encounter, from Auchtermuchty to Sauchiehall Street. This is not just a problem for incomers, however, as a native of Footdee (pronounced 'Fit-i') may not know how to say Milngavie ('Mil-guy'), and vice versa.

Those who do manage to get their tongues around the likes of Ecclefechan, Kirkintilloch, or Achiltibuie may wonder how these jawbreakers came into being. Like anywhere else, in Scotland names of places depend on the language spoken by the people who decided what to call them. Apart from English, the main influences have been Celtic and Scandinavian. Among the earliest inhabitants to have left a linguistic mark on the landscape were the Celtic people called Picts. Little is known about their language but it seems that any place name beginning with *Pit-* (Pittenweem, Pitsligo, Pitlochry) is of Pictish origin.

The later Celts, especially the Scots (who confusingly enough came from Ireland), handed down many common topographical terms. From their language (Gaelic) come the well-known *Ben* (mountain), *Loch* (lake, or arm of the sea), *Glen* (narrow valley), *Strath (broad valley)*, as well as *Ard-* (headland) and *Bal-* (hamlet).

Similarly, the Vikings contributed such endings as *-ay*, or *-a* (meaning island, as in Bernera and Westray), and *-ay* or *-wick* (meaning bay, as in Stornoway and Lerwick).

Deciphering local place names can be a fun way to while away a wet afternoon, but care must be taken not to jump to conclusions. Bathgate has nothing to do with baths, Ullapool is not named after a pool, and Gleneagles is unconnected with with birds of prey but rather means 'the glen of the church' (*eaglais* being the Gaelic word for a church).

**heart-roasted** (*pronounced* hart-**roe**-stit) *adjective spoken in Glasgow area* greatly tormented, frustrated, or worried: *He's got his aul mother heart-roasted wi' his wild behaviour.*

**heedrum-hodrum** (*pronounced* hee-drum-**hoe**-drum) *noun* traditional Gaelic singing or music, as disparaged by unappreciative Lowlanders: *Every Hogmanay we're expected to sit through all this heedrum-hodrum on the telly.* [an attempt to imitate the alleged sound of such music]

**heehaw** (*pronounced* hee-**haw**) *noun spoken in Glasgow* not the slightest bit or nothing at all: *Just you keep yer nose out of this. You know heehaw about it.*

[euphemistic rhyming slang for *damn a'*, *bugger a'*, etc]

**heid billydackus** (*pronounced* bil-ee-**dak**-uss) *or* **heid pilliedacus** (*pronounced* pil-ee-**dak**-uss) *noun spoken in East* a jocular, even derogatory, name for the person in charge of something [possibly from *billy*, an old word for a man or a workmate, plus a mock Latin ending]

**heidie** (*pronounced* **hee**-di) *noun* **1** an informal name for the head teacher of a school: *the heidie of an Ayrshire secondary school* **2** an act of striking a football with the head: *The first goal was a divin' heidie.* | *verb* to strike a football with one's head: *He heidied it over the bar.*

**hems** *noun* To **put the hems on**
something is to control, restrain or put
a stop to it: *The rain put the hems on our
trip to the seaside.* To **put the hems on**
someone is to make them behave in a
more restrained or moderate way: *She
used to go out with her pals every night, but
having that wean's really put the hems on
her.* [a **hem** or **haim** was part of the collar
put on a working horse]

**heuchter-teuchter** (*pronounced*
hooCH-ter-**chooCH**-ter) *adjective* a
derogatory description of Scottish folk
and country dance music: *Every time I
turn on the radio it's that heuchter-teuchter
rubbish.* [probably from a duplication of
**teuchter** a mildly derogatory word for a
Highlander]

**Hielan** (*pronounced* **heel**-an) *adjective*
**1** Highland: *Munro's much-loved stories about a daft Hielan skipper and a crabbit engineer.* **2** naive, gullible or a bit stupid: *That's a Hielan way of doing things; Ye'll no fool me. I'm no sae Hielan.*

**high heid yin** (*pronounced* hie-**heed**-yin) *noun* a person in a position of power or authority: *politicians, journalists and academics – opinion-shaping high heid yins in general*

**hine** *or* **hine awa** *adverb spoken in Northeast* far away: *hine ayont the braes; They'll be hine awa.*

**hin-end** (*pronounced* hin-**end** or hin-**en**) *noun* **1** the back, rear, or last section of something: *I might've known you'd turn* *up at the hin-end o' the day.* **2** a person's backside: *You might tidy up your stuff instead of leaving it all at your hin-end.*

**hingy** (*pronounced* **hing**-i) *adjective* slightly unwell and looking for sympathy or attention: *Jordan's been a bit hingy all day.* [from the idea of a sick child hanging on to a parent]

**hirple** *verb* to limp: *He hirpled off injured midway through the second half.* | *noun* a limp: *She's still walking with a bit of a hirple.*

**hoatching** *adjective* very busy, crowded, or full of something: *Largs is always hoatching on a holiday Monday; The island was hoatching with midges.*

**hochmagandy** *or* **houghmagandie**

(*pronounced* hoCH-ma-**gan**-dee) *noun* a jocular or poetic word for sexual intercourse outside marriage: *I wouldnae be surprised if there was a wee bit o' hochmagandy gaun on there.*

**Hogmanay** (*pronounced* hog-ma-**nay** or hug-ma-**nay**) *noun* the 31st of December, New Year's Eve: *BBC Scotland's Hogmanay show, Hogmanay Live, was watched by 1.2 million viewers.* [ultimately from Old French **aguillanneuf** a New Year's Eve gift]

**hoolet** (*pronounced* **hoo**-lit) *noun* an owl: *woods haunted by the hoolet's cry* [French **hulotte** an owl]

**hoor** *noun* **1** literally, a prostitute; but the word is often used as an offensive term for any woman: *He's running around wi' some wee hoor fae Fife; Shut up, ye auld hoor!* **2** any unpleasant person or thing: *We'd a hoor o' a job gettin it clean.* [Scots form of **whore**]

**hoose** (*pronounced* **hooss**) *noun* a house: *Come ben the hoose.*

**horny-golach** (*pronounced* hor-nee-**gol**-aCH) *noun spoken in Northeast* an earwig: *It's only an earwig, what my grannie used to call a horny-golach.* [see **golach**]

**hough** (*pronounced* **hawCH**) *noun* a joint of meat cut from the shin of the pig or cow: *Fling a ham hough intae the soup tae gie it flavour.* [Old English *hōh* meaning heel]

**howe** (*pronounced* **how**) *noun* a depression or hollow in the landscape, an area of low-lying land surrounded by hills (sometimes used in place names): *the Howe of Fife*

**howff** (*pronounced* **howf**) *noun* a place, especially a pub, used as a regular meeting place: *a lively musical howff with excellent real ale* [probably Dutch or Flemish *hof* a courtyard or enclosed space]

**howk** (*pronounced* **howk**) *verb* to extract something by, or as if by, digging or scraping: *We saw a few locals exercising their right to howk for cockles by hand and bucket; ballads howked from a spare and hostile landscape* [from old Low German]

79

**The Auld Alliance**

The Auld Alliance is the term used to categorize the historical links between Scotland and France. These links arose from a period of history when both countries were interested in securing an ally against England, their common powerful and expansionist neighbour. Various treaties between the two nations were in force from 1295 until the sixteenth century, when the Protestant Reformation left Scotland on the other side of the religious divide from Catholic France. During this period many Scots fought in France against the English, some even forming a bodyguard to the French king (the *Garde Écossais*) and French troops also served in Scotland. It was in order to fulfil the alliance with France that James IV launched the attack on England that led to his disastrous defeat at Flodden in 1513. Mary, Queen of Scots not only had a French mother (Mary of Guise) but had as her first husband the French Dauphin.

The laws and institutions of Scotland, as well as the country's customs and manners, were greatly influenced by the connection. The Scots were great importers of French wine, especially the claret of Bordeaux, and were given more favourable terms, as well as a higher-quality product, than English merchants. Interestingly enough, this wine trade, primarily through the port of Leith, seems to have been relatively undisturbed by the upheavals of the Reformation.

Another area of French influence was on the Scots language, and among the terms that can be traced back to French are *ashet* (from French *assiette*), *corbie* (from French *corbin*), *fash* (from French *facher*), *jalouse* (from French *jalouser*) and *merle* (which means a blackbird, just the same as in French).

**howtowdie** (*pronounced* how-**tow**-dee)
*noun* a dish of boiled chicken with
spinach and poached eggs: *Chicken
forms the basis of both cock-a-leekie and
howtowdie.* [from Old French *hétoudeau*
or *estaudeau* a fat young chicken for
cooking]

**huckle** *verb spoken in Glasgow* to force
someone to move by manhandling them
or bundling them roughly: *I huckled her
out the door before she could say anything
else.*

**hudderie** (*pronounced* **hud**-er-i) *adjective*
untidy or scruffy: *Yer hair's awfy hudderie
lookin, is it no?*

**humph** *verb* to carry something heavy:
*The main problem with living in a top flat*

*is having to humph your messages up three flights of stairs.*

**hurdies** *plural noun* the buttocks and hips: *He doesnae watch Nigella for the cookin. 'Fine strong hurdies' he aye says.*

**hurl** *noun* a lift or journey in a car or other motor vehicle: *Any chance of a hurl into town?*

**hyter** (*pronounced* **hie**-ter) *verb spoken in Northeast* to stumble or lurch: *He went hyterin aff tae his bed.*

**ill-trickit** (*pronounced* il-**trik**-it) *adjective spoken in Northeast* naughty or mischievous: *an ill-trickit bairn*

**ingin** *or* **ingan** (*pronounced* **ing**-in) *noun* an onion: *See's two pun o' ingins.*

83

**intimmers** (*pronounced* in-**tim**-merz)
*plural noun  spoken in Northeast* the
insides, of practically anything from the
internal workings of a clock to a person's
stomach and intestines: *Ah doot there's
somethin' no quite right in ma intimmers.*
[originally the internal **timbers** of a ship's
hull]

**jag**  *verb*  to prick something: *He jagged
his hand on the barbed wire.*  | *noun*  an
instance of being pricked or, most
usually, a jab or injection: *The wean got a
jag at school the day.*

**jaggy**  *adjective*  prickly or pointed: *There's
something jaggy in my shoe.*  | *noun*  a
stinging nettle: *She fell in the jaggies and
ran hame greetin.*

**jalouse** (*pronounced* ja-**looz**) *verb* to suspect or infer: *I jaloused ye'd be wantin yer tea.*

**jannie** *noun* a school janitor or caretaker: *Run and ask the jannie for the spare key.*

**jaup** (*pronounced* **jop**) *verb* to splash or spatter: *His breeks were a' jaupit wi mud fae the fields.* | *noun* a splash or spilt drop: *Don't get jaups of paint on my good carpet.*

**jawbox** *noun* a kitchen sink: *Ye'll get Vim and a cloth in ablow the jawbox.* [perhaps from the Scots *jaw* meaning to splash or pour]

**jenny-a'-things** (*pronounced* jen-nee-**aw**-thingz) *noun* a small shop selling a wide variety of goods: *Awa' an' see if the jenny-a'-things is open yet.*

> The term literally refers
> to an establishment run
> by a woman and selling
> everything you could desire.

**jenny longlegs**  *noun*  a crane fly:
*Daddy, there's a big jenny longlegs in my bedroom.*

**jessie**  *noun*  an effeminate, weak, or cowardly man: *What are ye greetin for, ye big jessie?*; *Shinty is not a game for jessies.*

> It is not clear why this
> particular girls' name was
> chosen for this use, or indeed
> whether Scottish women
> called Jessie were historically

any feebler than your average
Mary or Margaret.

**jing-bang** (*pronounced* jing-**bang**)
*noun* the whole lot or everything: *Ah'm
scunnered wi' the hale jing-bang o' them.*

**jings** *interjection* an exclamation of mild
surprise: *Jings! I didn't know we weren't
supposed to sit here.*

> This exclamation might not
> have become so common
> had it not been immortalized
> by Scotland's most famous
> cartoon family, The Broons.

**jink** *verb* to move swiftly or jerkily or
make a quick turn in order to dodge: *He
jinked through from 20 metres out for a
superb individual try.*

**jouk** (*pronounced* **jook**) *verb* to duck or dodge: *She jouked out the way of the snowball.* | *noun* a sudden evasive movement: *With a sudden jouk up a close the cat left her pursuers behind.*

**keech** (*pronounced* **keeCH**) *noun* excrement: *Ah've gone and stood on a dog's keech.*

**keelie** (*pronounced* **keel**-i) *noun* a young working-class person from a city or large town, especially Glasgow: *She married a right Glesca keelie.* [from Gaelic **gille** a lad]

> You have to be careful in using this term. To many people it is derogatory and will be taken as an insult

implying being rough and uncultured. On the other hand, some individuals, particularly Glaswegians, will proudly describe themselves as keelies.

**kenspeckle** *adjective* familiar, well-known, or easily recognized: *He is a kenspeckle figure in Edinburgh's Asian community.* [perhaps from Old Norse **kennispecki** power of recognition]

**kist** *noun* a large chest or wooden box: *This is the kist where they used to keep sheets and blankets.*

**kittle** or **kittlie** *adjective* unpredictable and capricious: *He's aye been kittle tae deal wi'.* | *verb* **1** to be puzzling or troubling to someone: *That's something that kittles me yet.* **2** to tickle or be ticklish: *Stop kittlin the weans or they'll never go down the night.*

**knowe** or **know** (*pronounced* **now**) *noun* a small rounded hill: *Ca' the yowes tae the knowes.* [a Scots form of ***knoll***]

**knype on** (*pronounced* **nipe**) *verb spoken in Northeast* to keep going or slog away at something, often used in the sense of going steadily through life without any great mishap: *Aye knypin on?* [***Knype*** literally means to knock]

**kye** *plural noun* cattle: *The kye are in the byre.*

**lade** *noun* a watercourse, especially one that carries water to a mill: *The old mill* lade off the River Leithen powered five woollen mills and a saw-mill.

**laich** or **laigh** (*pronounced* **layCH**) *adjective* low: *a laich whisper*

**laird** *noun* a lord, especially the owner of a large estate: *a sixteenth-century laird's mansion*

**laldie** or **laldy** (*pronounced* **lal**-dee) *noun* To **give it laldie** means to do something vigorously: *Down one end of the room there was a gang of folkies giving it laldy, and good foot-tapping music filled the bar.*

**laverock** (*pronounced* **lav**-er-ok or **layv**-rok) *noun* a skylark (the bird): *We could hear a laverock singing somewhere high above.*

**law** *noun spoken in Lowlands* a hill, especially a rounded one (often used as part of a place name): *Broad Law; Dundee Law* | *adjective* low: *the law, law lands o' Holland*

**leet** *noun* a list of candidates for a job, award, contract, etc: *She was on the short leet of four applicants interviewed on May 21.*

**leid** (*pronounced* **leed**) *noun* a chiefly literary word for a language: *the auld Scots leid* [Old English]

**linn** *noun* a waterfall or the pool at the foot of one: *A couple of anglers were trying their luck on the linn.* [from the Gaelic *linne* a pool and the Old English *hlynn* a torrent]

**lintie** *noun* a linnet: *singin like a lintie*

**lippen** *verb* to trust or depend on: *Ye maunna lippen til him.*

**loon** or **loun** *noun spoken in Northeast* a boy or lad: *He was a local loon, born and bred in Aberdeen.*

> It is worth noting that in Northest Scotland calling someone a loon does not indicate that you think they are a fool - at least, not necessarily.

**loup** or **lowp** (*pronounced* **lowp**) *verb* to leap or jump: *If you wait long enough, you might see a salmon louping.* | *noun* a leap or jump: *He cleared the dyke with one great loup.*

## The written word

The history of Scottish literature is dominated by two towering figures: Robert Burns and Sir Walter Scott.

Burns was an Ayrshire farmer's son who achieved instant fame when in 1786 his *Poems, Chiefly in the Scottish Dialect* was published. His verse ranged from biting satire, such as 'Holy Willie's Prayer', to the racy comic narrative of 'Tam O'Shanter', to the tenderest of love lyrics like 'O my luve's like a red, red rose'. He is remembered every year on his birthday, January 25th, at Burns Suppers, where various carryings-on involving bagpipes and haggis, that would probably have puzzled him, are solemnly enacted.

As a youth Scott met and was impressed by Burns and he wrote much verse himself, but it is as a novelist that he is most celebrated, with such titles as *Waverley, Rob Roy* and *Ivanhoe* pouring from his fecund pen. It has to be said that nowadays the works of Scott are studied as an academic exercise rather than read for pleasure.

Yet there are many other Scottish writers of importance. Robert Louis Stevenson was perhaps Scott's true heir, with gripping historical fiction such as *Catriona*, but his *Strange Case of Dr Jekyll and Mr Hyde* not only enthralled the reading public but gave the English language a new expression.

In the twentieth century Scottish writing developed in many directions, with poets like Hugh MacDiarmid writing in Scots, Sorley McLean in Gaelic, and Edwin Morgan defying narrow classification. The novel flourished, with exponents like Neil Gunn, Lewis Grassic Gibbon, Robin Jenkins, and James Kelman dealing with the realities of everyday Scottish life, and Alasdair Gray veering off into the fantastical.

Today's Scottish bestsellers range from the gentle satire of Alexander McCall Smith to the dark musings of Ian Rankin in his *Rebus* police novels.

**lowse** (*pronounced* **lowss**) *adjective*
loose: *Is this skirt no a bit lowse?* | *verb*
**1** to loose or release something: *Doon
she lowsed her bonny black hair.* **2** to
finish work: *They lowse at five o'clock.*
***Lowsin time*** is the time at which work or
school finishes: *I'll get ye at the gate at
lowsin time.*

**lum** *noun* a chimney: *Run next door
and tell them their lum's on fire!* The
traditional saying **lang may your lum reek**
(literally, long may your chimney smoke)
is a way of wishing someone long life
and prosperity

**machair** (*pronounced* **maCH**-er) *noun*
a type of low-lying sandy grassy land
found just above the high-water mark
of many sandy shores in western

Scotland, particularly in the Hebrides.
It is often more fertile than the more
mountainous areas further inland:
*unspoilt miles of machair, beach, and
headland*  [Gaelic]

> Machair is such a
> distinctive element of
> Hebridean life that the
> word was used as the title
> of a Gaelic-language soap
> opera set on the Isle of
> Lewis, first broadcast on
> Scottish Television in the
> 1990s.

**maddie**  *noun*  a wild or crazy person:
*Tell that maddie tae stop shoutin an
bawlin.*

**makar** (*pronounced* **mak**-er) *noun* a poet: *a grand meetin o' a' the makars*

> While this is chiefly an old-fashioned or literary word, it was used as recently as 2004 when Edwin Morgan was named as the first Scots Makar, or national poet of Scotland.

**malky** (*pronounced* **mal**-kee) *spoken in Glasgow* *noun* a slang term for a razor used as a weapon: *She used to take his malky into the dancehall for him in her handbag.* | *verb* to slash someone with a razor: *A boy got malkied in there last night.*

> Apparently this comes from rhyming slang for Malcolm Fraser, but the identity of

this individual has been lost
in the mists of time and
booze. He is certainly not to
be identified with the former
Australian prime minister of
that name.

**mannie** *noun* **1** any man: *the mannie
from the gas board* **2** *spoken in Northeast*
the man in charge of something,
especially if he is also its owner, for
instance a farmer or the skipper of a
fishing boat

**mappie-mou** (*pronounced* map-ee-
**moo**) *noun spoken in Northeast* the
antirrhinum or snapdragon: *a braw
display o' mappie-mous in the front
gairden* [from *mappie*, a pet name for a
rabbit, plus *mou* mouth]

**The romance of the Jacobites**

The Jacobites were the supporters of King James II (and his heirs), after he had been deposed by William of Orange in 1688, and they took part in armed revolts in Scotland more than once. However, it is the last great uprising of 1745-6 that is thought of by most people as *the* Jacobite Rebellion.

In 1745 the grandson of James II, Charles Edward Stuart, (also known to history as the Young Pretender and to romance as Bonnie Prince Charlie) raised his standard at Glenfinnan and called on the Highland clans to rally to his cause. Some did and others didn't, but the Jacobite army marched south, defeating a government force at Prestonpans. Crossing into England, they reached Derby before, having failed to gather expected support from English Jacobites, they felt obliged to retreat and headed back into Scotland. Their much-depleted army was eventually crushed by government forces at Culloden and a severe campaign of repression followed in the Highlands.

These are the facts, but they are often obscured in popular imagination. Many believe that the battle of Culloden was a confrontation between England and Scotland, but there were many Scots, in both Lowland British Army regiments and Highland clans, fighting on the government side against what they saw as representatives of Catholic tyranny. Most of Lowland Scotland would have been glad to see the end of the threat to their way of life from the Highlands. But, as often happens, the legend is more attractive than the truth and the cherished stories of Bonnie Prince Charlie's flight in the heather and his rescue by Flora MacDonald continue to outshine mere historical fact.

**maun** (*pronounced* **mawn**) *verb* must:
*He maun hae dropped it.*

**mawkit** *adjective spoken in West
Central* **1** very dirty: *a mawkit semmit*
**2** offensively bad: *That singing's mawkit!*
[literally, infested with maggots, from
*mauk*, an old Scots name for a
maggot]

**meen** *noun spoken in Northeast* the
moon: *Oot frae the clouds came the
bonnie meen.*

**meenit** *noun* a minute: *It's only five
meenits tae lowsin time.*

**meggy-mony-feet** (*pronounced* meg-
ee-**mun**-nee-feet) *noun* a centipede

**meikle** (*pronounced* **meek**-il) *adjective*

big or large (often found in place names): *Meikle Earnock*

**meiny** (*pronounced* **may**-nee) *noun spoken in Northeast* a disparaging word for a crowd or large group of people; a rabble: *amang the meiny in Union Street* [from Old French]

**merse** (*pronounced* **merss**) *noun spoken in South* an area of low-lying fertile land near a river or shore: *the peaceful sight of cattle grazing on the merse* **The Merse** is a low-lying fertile region in the Eastern Borders, between the River Tweed and the Lammermuir Hills [Old English, meaning marsh]

**messan** (*pronounced* **mess**-an) *noun spoken in Central & South* an obnoxious or contemptible person: *Stop that right now, ye dirty wee messan!* [ultimately from Gaelic **measan** meaning small dog]

**midden** *noun* **1** the area at the back of a block of flats where the communal dustbins are kept: *Ye cannae stop weans playin in the midden.* **2** a dunghill: *the reek o' the midden by the byre* **3** any dirty or untidy person or thing: *Are you ever going to clean this place up, ye dirty auld midden?*; *This room's a right midden.*

**midgie** (*pronounced* **mij**-ee) *noun* **1** a midge: *The midgies were out in force and we soon retreated indoors.* **2** a dustbin or litter bin: *An old tramp was raking through the midgies.* [sense 2 comes from the word **midden**]

**ming** *verb* to smell strongly and unpleasantly: *It's great to be able to go to the pub and not come home minging of cigarette smoke.* | *noun* a strong unpleasant smell or stink: *There's a right ming coming from the fridge.*

**mink** *or* **minker** *noun spoken in East* a scruffy or disreputable person: *He's away oot dressed lik a minker.* [from Gaelic *muince* a collar, figuratively used to mean a noose and implying that the person referred to would be, to quote the 19th-century judge Lord Braxfield, "nane the waur o' a hanging"]

**minky** *adjective spoken in East* dirty or disgusting: *Have you no cleaned those minky shoes yet?*; *Having to go out begging made me feel all minky.*

**mixter-maxter** (*pronounced* mik-ster-mak-ster) *or* **mixtie-maxtie** *adjective, adverb* in an untidy jumbled way: *Papers were strewn mixter-maxter across the desk.* | *noun* a confused jumble: *The film contains a mixter-maxter of inadequately thought out ideas.*

**mochie** *or* **mochy** (*pronounced* moCH-ee) *adjective* damp, misty, and unpleasantly humid: *It's awfy mochie weather we hae the noo.* [from Old Norse *mugga* mist]

**mollach** (*pronounced* **mol**-aCH) *verb spoken in Northeast* to hang around or wander about aimlessly: *Fit are ye mollachin aboot at?* [from the behaviour of *moles*, in throwing up molehills apparently at random]

**moothie** *noun* a mouth-organ or harmonica: *He's one of the best moothie players in all Scotland.*

**mowdie** *or* **mowdiewart** (*pronounced* **mow**-dee-wort) *noun* a mole (the animal): *I see the mowdies have been busy in your back garden.* [from **moldewarpe**, literally earth-thrower, an archaic name for a mole]

**nabbler** *noun* spoken in Northeast a fast and skilful worker: *Ye can mak guid money, gin ye're a nabbler.*

**nae** (*pronounced* **nay**) *adjective* no or not: *There's nae mair; She'll nae be back yet.*

**nash** *verb* spoken in Edinburgh area to hurry or dash: *I'll just nash along to the shop for a paper.* [Romany]

**ned** *noun spoken in Glasgow area* a young male hooligan or petty criminal: *He's a right wee ned.* [shortened from Edward, perhaps related to teddy boy]

**nedette** (*pronounced* ned-**et**) *noun spoken in Glasgow area* a female ned: *nedettes in their muffin tops*

**neep** *noun* a turnip: *The farmhands are lifting neeps.*

**Ne'erday** (*pronounced* **nair**-day) *noun* New Year's Day: *the Ne'erday television highlights*

**neuk** (*pronounced* **nyook**) *noun* **1** a corner or nook: *sitting in a neuk by the fire* **2** an area of land that projects into the sea: *the East Neuk of Fife*

**numpty** *noun  spoken in Glasgow area*  a stupid person: *That's no the way to do it, ya numpty!*

**nyaff** (*pronounced* n-**yaff**) *noun*  a worthless or irritating person, especially a small one: *Never mind what that wee nyaff says.* [perhaps an imitation of the barking of a small dog]

**oose** (*pronounced* **ooss**) *noun*  dust or fluff: *Have you seen the oose under that bed?* [originally the plural of **oo**, a Scots word for wool]

**orra** (*pronounced* **or**-ra *or* **or**-ree) *adjective  spoken in Tayside & Northeast* coarse or uncouth in behaviour or speech: *When she talks like that we feel all orra and common.*  On a traditional

Scottish farm, an **orraman, orra lad,** or (in the Northeast) **orra loon** was a man or boy employed to do miscellaneous unskilled work: *Leave that til the orraman.* [perhaps from **ower a'** over all, everywhere or general]

**ower** (*pronounced* **ow**-er) *preposition* over: *He flung it ower the wa'.* | *adverb* too or excessively: *It's ower warm for a jumper.*

**owergyaan** (*pronounced* owr-**gyahn**) *or* **owergan** (*pronounced* owr-**gan**) *noun spoken in Northeast* a scolding or telling-off: *a gweed owergyaan* [Compare the English **going-over**, a scolding or thrashing]

**oxter** *noun* an armpit: *Ah'm up tae ma oxters in work the noo.*

**pap** *verb* to throw: *Pap that in the bucket, will you?*; *He got papped out of the Uni after failing his resits.* | *noun* **1** a female breast: *a bairn at the pap* **2** used in the name of various conical, roughly breast-shaped, hills: *the Paps of Jura*

**partan** (*pronounced* **par**-tan) *noun* a crab, especially a common edible crab, often made into a soup called *partan bree*: *There was no lobster in the creel, only a couple of partans.* [Gaelic]

**pawkie** *or* **pawky** (*pronounced* **paw**-ki) *adjective* showing a dry sense of humour, especially when a shrewd and down-to-earth criticism of hypocrisy or pretension is involved: *learned enthusiasm sprinkled with a pawky sense of humour* [from the earlier *pawk* a trick]

### It's the law

Non-Scottish viewers of TV cop shows such as *Rebus* or *Taggart* may be puzzled not only by the broad accents and dialogue but also by some of the legal language that is casually flung about. Of course, law-abiding folk should have no practical involvement in these matters, but a little information is always welcome to the curious.

When Scotland became part of the United Kingdom in 1707, one of the Scottish institutions that lived on was the distinctive Scots legal system. In historical terms, the main difference between Scots law and English law is that the former is based on Roman law, while in England common law, based on precedent, underpins the legal system. This is not to say that you can get away with your favourite crimes in one part of the United Kingdom and not in another; it's more about the terminology.

In Scotland a barrister is known as an 'advocate', a public prosecutor is called a 'Procurator Fiscal', and the accused is referred to as the 'panel'. Someone who claims to have committed GBH north of the border is not being strictly accurate; in Scotland this would be called 'assault'. Similarly, people who are deliberately careless with matches or cans of petrol would not be guilty of arson but of 'wilful fire-raising' and manslaughter is known as 'culpable homicide'. A particularly notable element of Scots law is the concept of 'not proven', the famous 'third verdict' available to a Scottish jury when there is insufficient evidence for a conviction, or, as some would have it, 'we know you did it but we can't prove it'.

**pech** (*pronounced* **peCH**) *verb* to pant
for breath, especially after exerting
yourself: *We were all peching by the time
we reached the top.* **peched out** means
exhausted and out of breath: *I was that
peched out I had to sit down.*

**peedie** *adjective spoken in Orkney &
Caithness* small: *just a peedie boy*

**peely-wally** or **peelie-wallie**
(*pronounced* pee-lee-**wal**-lee) *adjective*
**1** pale and unhealthy-looking: *She says
she's fine but she looks peely-wally to
me.* **2** lacking in the desired strength or
vigour: *This tea's a bit peely-wally.*

**peenge** *verb* to moan or complain in
a whining, peevish manner: *Stop your
peengeing, we've only got a little further to go.*

114

**peerie heels** *plural noun spoken in Central & South* stiletto heels: *peerie heels and pointed toes* [from **peerie** meaning small]

**perjink** (*pronounced* per-**jink**) *adjective* neat and precise about things to the point of being fussy or prim: *She's awful perjink about her appearance.*

**photie** *noun* a photograph: *Staun ower there till I take yer photie.*

**piece** *noun* a sandwich or slice of bread eaten as part of a packed lunch or as a snack: *We sat on a bench to eat our pieces; a piece and cheese*

**pinkie** *noun* the little finger: *I'm practising drinking coffee with my pinkie in the air.* [from Dutch **pink** little finger]

**pish** *noun, verb* a euphemism for 'piss': *Ah'm away for a pish; It was pishing down outside.* | *adjective* of very poor quality: *Okay, it was a pish programme, but we enjoyed appearing on it.* Someone who is **pished** is drunk: *She wis pished oot her brain.*

> This term is quite playful and would be regarded as inoffensive by most Scots.

**plank** *verb* 1 to put something away somewhere safe or hidden for later use: *The old man's got a few cans planked away somewhere.* 2 to place or put something down in a forceful manner: *He planked the file down on the desk in front of me.* | *noun* a secret supply or

116

cache of something: *His mum found a plank of jazz mags under his bed.*

**playpiece** *noun* any snack, such as a biscuit, a packet of crisps, or an apple, that a child takes to school to eat during the morning break or interval: *The wean's away tae school withoot her playpiece.*

**plettie** *noun spoken in Dundee* a balcony or landing in a block of flats: *sittin oot on the plettie drinkin a can ae export* [from *plat* meaning flat or level]

**plook** or **plouk** *noun* a pimple: *That's him there, the wan wi' plooks a' ower his face.*

**plooky** or **plookit** *adjective* having a lot of pimples: *I'm too plooky to go out the night.*

**plouter** (*pronounced* **plow**-ter) *verb* to splash through, or play about with, water or mud: *The bairns were havin' a rare time plowterin' through the puddles.*

**plump** *noun* a sudden, heavy fall of rain: *Take your brolly; there's going to be a plump.*

**pochle** *or* **pauchle** (*pronounced* **poCH**-l) *verb* to dishonestly rig or fix something so that a particular result is obtained: *He is widely believed to be the man who pochled the election; To some people it is "creative accountancy", to others it is simply pochling the books.* | *noun* an instance of cheating; a swindle or fiddle: *The chairman's wife won first prize in the raffle: talk about a pochle!* [from the Old Scots **pakkald**, ultimately from **pack** a bundle]

**pook** *noun* a tuft of hair, wool, etc. sticking out from something: *There's a pook on your jumper.*

**port-a-beul** (*pronounced* **porsh**-ta-**bee**-al) *noun* the singing of simple or meaningless words to a tune originally intended as purely instrumental music: *He won a medal at the Mod for his port-a-beul.* [Gaelic, meaning music from mouth]

**prig** *verb spoken in North* to beg, plead, or beseech: *It had taken a lot of prigging to get her to go.*

**prog** *verb* to pierce or prick something, or to stick something pointed into it: *I always prog the ham with cloves before cooking it.*

## A taste of Scotland

Scotland is reputed to be the home of the near-mythical deep-fried Mars Bar, and the west in particular is renowned for a diet dangerous to both the teeth and the heart. The great English lexicographer Samuel Johnson famously defined oats as 'a grain, which in England is generally given to horses, but in Scotland supports the people'. While Dr Johnson was no doubt indulging in one of his favourite pastimes – Scot-baiting – it is true that oats have always been important in the Scots diet, from porridge to oatcakes. The other dish that is considered typically Scottish is of course haggis, although many Scots never taste this delicacy from one year's end to the next. If it didn't exist it would have to be invented, if only for the endless pleasure derived by natives teasing tourists about how the haggis is hunted in the glens.

Restaurants that specialize in Scottish cooking are becoming increasingly common, and it is possible to fill a reasonable menu with 'national' dishes. Typical soups include Scotch broth and cockieleekie. For a main dish, you might order a gigot chop, howtowdie or venison, accompanied by neeps and tatties. Local cheeses include crowdie and caboc, and those with a sweet tooth could round off the meal with clootie dumpling or cranachan.

Before such restaurants emerged, Scotland had long taken to Indian and Pakistani food in a big way. Many Scots in exile from the motherland find themselves pining not so much for haggis as a good curry, or even that most cutting-edge of fusion dishes, a pakora supper.

Menu
haggis
neeps & tatties
claggum
stovies
porridge
battered batter
gross obesity
heart attacks

**puddock** *noun* a frog or toad: *She found a wee orange puddock in the back garden.* [from Old English *pad* a toad]

**puggy** *or* **puggie** *noun* **1** a fruit machine or one-armed bandit: *He lost all his cash on the puggy.* **2** a cash-dispenser machine: *Sorry I took so long; there was some queue at the puggy.* **3** an old name for a monkey: *Anybody ever tell ye ye've got a face like a puggie?* The saying *fou as a puggie* means very drunk To *get your puggie up* or *take a puggie* means to lose one's temper: *He took a puggie an flung his mobile oot the windae.*

**purvey** (*pronounced* **per**-vee) *noun* the food and drink provided after a funeral, at a wedding reception, etc.: *There'll be a bit of a purvey at the Miners' Welfare* *afterwards.* [from Old French **porveeir** to provide]

**quaich** (*pronounced* **kwayCH**) *noun* a small shallow drinking cup, usually with two handles, nowadays mostly used as ornaments or trophies: *He gave his best man a fine silver quaich.* [Gaelic **cuach** cup]

**queenie** *noun* a type of shellfish (a queen scallop): *a stew of squid, queenies, monkfish, and crab*

**queet** *noun spoken in Northeast* an ankle: *She strained her queet.* [from older Scots **cuit**, which comes from Middle Dutch]

**quine** (*pronounced* **kwine**) *or* **quean** (*pronounced* **kween**) *noun spoken in*

*Northeast* a young unmarried woman or girl: *He had mairrit on a quine fae Torry.* [Old English]

**radge** *or* **raj** *or* **radgie** *or* **rajie**
*spoken in Edinburgh & East* *adjective*
To be or go **radge** is to act in a wild or crazy way: *He went totally radge when he heard what I'd done; Stop that, ya rajie wee bastard!* | *noun* someone who behaves in a wild or irrational way: *D'ye ken whit the radge did next?* [probably a variant of *rage*, although it may be influenced by the Romany *raj* stupid or crazy]

**raggle** *noun* a groove cut in a piece of stone or wood to enable another piece to fit into it: *This is the raggle that was cut to take the roof.* | *verb* to cut such a groove in a piece of stone or wood: *Raggling the walls makes a real mess.*

**raivel** (*pronounced* **ray**-vel) *verb* **1** to become tangled or confused: *Dinna let the cat raivel yer knittin'; The fishin' lines are a' raivelt.* **2** to baffle or confuse: *His mind's aa raivelt.*

**rammy** *noun* a noisy fight or brawl: *Tempers flared, leading to a rammy involving groups of youths from the two towns.*

**ramstam** (*pronounced* ram-**stam**) *adverb, adjective* in a hurried and clumsy way, without proper care or thought: *She aye goes at it ramstam.*

**randan** (*pronounced* ran-**dan**) *noun* a spree or a wild or dissolute good time, frequently but not necessarily one involving heavy drinking: *They were out on the randan to celebrate the end of term.* [probably from **random**]

**rax** *verb* **1** to stretch your body or a part of your body: *He raxed out his arm.* **2** to fetch something or give it to someone else with an outstretched arm: *Rax us ower the salt.* **3** to sprain or wrench a limb by stretching or turning it too far or too energetically: *He's aff work after raxin' his shoulder.* [Old English]

**redd** *verb* to clear or tidy up something: *I must get round to redding up that cupboard sometime.* | *noun* an act of tidying a place up: *We'll need to give the front room a good redd before your mother comes.*

**reese** (*pronounced* **reez**) *verb* *spoken in Northeast* to praise or extol: *He aye reesed the wifie's bannocks.*

**reestit** (*pronounced* **ree**-stit) *adjective spoken in Shetland* (referring to food) cured by drying or smoking: *Reestit mutton is a Shetland speciality, a type of wind-dried mutton used for making soup.* [probably Scandinavian]

**rickle** *noun* a loose heap or pile of things: *The old house was now just a rickle of stones.* To say someone is ***a rickle of banes*** is a picturesque way of saying that they are unhealthily thin [probably Scandinavian]

**rive** *verb* to pull or tug something firmly, or to tear it by pulling at it: *We rived at* the tree-stump but couldn't shift it. | *noun* a firm pull or tug: *He gie'd it such a rive that it came awa' in his haun.*

**roch** (*pronounced* **roCH**) *adjective* rough: *Yon's a gey roch pub.*

**ronepipe** *or* **rhonepipe** *noun* one of the drain pipes running from the gutter on a roof to the ground: *He was locked out, so he thought he'd climb up the ronepipe.*

**roup** (*pronounced* **rowp**) *noun* an auction: *They said goods and effects will be sold by public roup.*

**rowie** *noun spoken in Northeast* the type of flaky, butter-rich, bread roll, originally from Aberdeen, which is generally called a **buttery** elsewhere in Scotland: *and half a dozen rowies, please*

**rummlethump** (*pronounced* **rum**-l-thump) *or* **rummledethump** (*pronounced* **rum**-l-dee-thump) *noun* a dish made of cabbage mixed into mashed potatoes: *wild salmon on a bed of rummledethump*

**runkle** *verb* to crease or crumple something: *His jacket was all runkled when he took it down from the locker.*

**saftie** *noun* **1** *spoken in Northeast* a soft bread roll, a bap, as distinct from a **rowie**: *twa safties, twa rowies, and a French stick* **2** slippers are sometimes called **safties**: *The dug's awa' wi' ma safties again!*

**sair** *adjective* **1** aching and painful: *a sair heid* **2** difficult or requiring a lot of

129

effort: *Aye, it's a sair fecht havin tae work for a livin.*

**sannies** *plural noun* *spoken in Central* gym-shoes or plimsolls: *Do thae sannies still fit ye?* [shortened from **sandshoes**]

**sapple** *spoken in Central* *verb* to rinse something or wash it out: *Sapple that teapot till I put the kettle on again.* | *noun* soapy lather: *She plunged another cardie into the sapples.*

**scaffie** *or* **scaffy** *noun* a street-sweeper or dustman; often used as a term of abuse to imply that someone is dirty: *Ah wouldnae gie that clown a start as a scaffie; Away and put on a clean shirt, ya scaffie!* [shortened from **scavenger**]

**scart** *verb* to scratch or scrape: *Ah scartit ma heid on a branch.* | *noun* A **scart** is a scratch or scrape: *Oor hauns were a' scarts wi' pickin brambles; a well-fired roll wi' just a wee scart o' butter*

**schemie** (*pronounced* **skee**-mi) *noun* a person who lives on one of the large council housing estates (schemes) on the outskirts of many Scottish towns: *The bus was full of schemies heading into town for their Saturday night's entertainment.*

**sclaff** *verb* **1** to hit something, especially a ball, with a glancing blow: *The striker swung his boot at the loose ball but only succeeded in sclaffing it wide for a goal-kick.* **2** in golf, to mishit the ball because the head of the club has hit the ground a glancing blow before striking the ball:

*You wouldn't expect a player of her calibre to sclaff an approach shot.* | *noun* a slap or glancing blow, or a golf shot mishit as described above: *The branch swung back and gave him a sclaff on the ear.*

**sclim** *verb* to climb: *When I was wee I could sclim up that tree no bother.* (The past tense can be either **sclimmed** or **sclam**)

**scoosh** *or* **skoosh** *verb* to squirt or spurt: *He scooshed me with a water pistol; Water came scooshing out of the tap.* If you do something easily, without having to make a serious effort you might be said to **scoosh it**: *At home to Stenhousemuir in the next round? Ach, we'll scoosh it.* | *noun* **1** a squirt or spurt of liquid: *Put another wee scoosh of cream* *on it.* **2** any fizzy soft drink: *Ah could murder a can o' scoosh.* **3** something that is considered very easy to deal with (also **scoosh case**): *Buying a new house in the current market is easy, a scoosh case.*

**scud** *noun* a slap or smack: *Are you wanting a scud on the lug?* **In the scud** or, even more shockingly, **in the bare scud**, means naked: *She was wandering around the house in the bare scud.* | *verb* to slap or smack: *I'll scud your ear in a minute.*

**scunner** *verb* to irritate or disgust: *Behaviour like that scunners me, so it does.* **scunnered** means sickened or disgusted, either because something is unpleasant or because you are utterly fed up with it: *I'm scunnered with having to get up at six every morning.* | *noun* a feeling of disgust or loathing, or whatever causes this feeling: *I took a scunner to Shakespeare when I had to study him at Uni*; *This weather's a right scunner, isn't it?*

**selt** *verb* a Scottish past form of sell, often used instead of sold: *Have ye selt yer hoose yet?*

**semmit** *or* **simmit** (*pronounced* **sem**-mit *or* **sim**-mit) *noun* a vest: *No wonder you're cold. Away and put your semmit on.*

**sharger** (*pronounced* **sharg**-er) *noun spoken in Northeast* a weak, puny, or stunted-looking person or animal: *Nane o' my bairns hae been shargers.* [Gaelic *searg* a puny creature]

**shargert** (*pronounced* **sharg**-ert) *or* **shargered** (*pronounced* **sharg**-erd)

134

*adjective spoken in Northeast* weak, puny, or stunted looking: *a shargert-lookin' quine*

**sharn** *or* **shairn** *noun* dung, especially the dung of cattle: *sharn on his boots*

**shauchle** (*pronounced* **shawCH-l**) *verb* to walk slowly and awkwardly without lifting your feet properly: *Some old guy was shauchling along the street.*

**sheugh** *or* **sheuch** (*pronounced* **shuCH**) *noun* **1** a gutter or ditch for drainage: *a long sheugh which his father had dug with a pick and shovel* If you are said to be **up a sheugh** or **up the sheugh** you are completely mistaken or have the wrong idea entirely: *Ah doot we're up the sheuch this time.* **2** the entire area around the buttocks and genitals: *He's a wee dumpy guy – always looks as if his sheuch's too near the ground; sweaty sheuch syndrome, as experienced during driving tests* **3** more specifically, the cleft between the buttocks: *I could feel the sweat trickling into the sheuch o' my erse.* [from Middle English **sogh** a swamp]

**shilpit** (*pronounced* **shil**-pit) *adjective* thin and weak-looking, as if underfed or in poor health: *Who's that wee shilpit-lookin' creature next tae you in the photie?*

**shirrackin** *or* **sherrackin** (*pronounced* **sher**-rak-in) *noun spoken in Glasgow* a severe scolding or telling-off: *The weans got a right shirrackin for no sayin' where they were gaun.*

**shoogle** *verb* to shake, sway, or rock from side to side: *The trailer shoogled alarmingly as we drove up the track; He shoogled his son awake.* | *noun* a shake, push or nudge: *Give me a shoogle if it looks like I'm falling asleep.*

**shoogly** (*pronounced* **shoo**-gul-i) *adjective* shaky, unsteady or wobbly: *That's an awful shoogly table.* If your **jaicket is on a shoogly nail** or **peg** you are in danger of losing your job: *That's the second big order we've lost this month. The boss's jaicket must be on a shoogly peg.*

**shunky** *noun* a toilet: *I've just got time tae nip tae the shunky afore we go.*

The word may possibly come from Shanks & Co of

Barrhead, near Glasgow, a
well-known manufacturer of
ceramic ware whose brand-
name on their goods will
have impressed itself on
generations of grateful
users.

**simmer dim** *noun  spoken in Orkney
& Shetland*  the night-long twilight in
Orkney and Shetland in midsummer,
when dusk runs more or less directly
into dawn and it is never truly dark: *up
all night enjoying the simmer dim*

**skail** (*pronounced* **skayl**) *verb*  **1** if
someone says a building, such as a
factory, pub, or hall is *skailing*, it is
emptying at the end of a shift, closing
time, etc. You can also say that the

occupants are **skailing**: *The road's aye busy when the bingo's skailing; We were held up by the crowd skailin oot o' Murrayfield.* **2** to spill: *Watch you don't skail my pint!*

**skeich** (*pronounced* **skeeCH**) *adjective* **1** in an excited, lively but easily upset mood (often used of young children): *The bairns're ower skeich already wi'oot yon nonsense.* **2** fit and active: *The old mannie's as skeich as ony youngster.*

**skelf** *noun* **1** a splinter of wood, especially one embedded in your skin: *He was taking a skelf out of his thumb with a pin.* **2** a small thin person: *What does a wee skelf of a lassie like her need to diet for?*

### The water of life

There are other countries that produce whisky, but it was Scotland that gave the drink its name (from the Gaelic *uisgebeatha* meaning water of life), and the word 'Scotch' has become synonymous with whisky all around the world.

Scotch whisky can be made in several ways. Most bottles that are sold are 'blends', containing both grain whisky and malt whisky. These offer a taste that is acceptable to most palates at a price that is acceptable to most wallets. However, many of the most popular blended whiskies are treated with a certain disdain by Scotland's more discerning drinkers. Instead it is the single malt that offers most interest.

Single malts are distilled only from malted barley and are the products of a single distillery. This means that each has a distinctive character according to the materials used in the procedure.

There are distilleries all over Scotland, but Speyside is the home of half of the country's distilleries and many of the most famous and distinctive single malts, such as Knockando, Glenlivet, and Macallan. The island of Islay has seven distilleries and produces the famous malts Arbeg, Lagavulin, and Laphroaig.

For a drink that is meant to raise the spirits, whisky is treated with remarkable seriousness by many of its devotees. Conversations rumble on deep into the night about the relative qualities of different whiskies and the optimum conditions for drinking them. For other Scots, such questions are academic and any drop of the hard stuff will be sufficient to grace a special occasion such as Hogmanay or a Burns Supper.

**skelp** *noun* a smack or slap: *All that boy needs is a good skelp.* | *verb* **1** to smack or slap: *Ah hate tae see a mammy skelpin' her wean.* **2** to move or go quickly: *He went skelping down the road after the bus.*

**skiddle** *verb* to splash or spill water or another liquid or to play about splashily with water: *bairns skiddlin' in the paddlin' pool* | *noun* a wet splashed or spilled mess, or a period of time spent playing about with water: *Mop up that skiddle on the kitchen floor.*

**skinnymalink** (*pronounced* **skin**-ee-ma-link) *or* **skinnymalinkie** (*pronounced* skin-ee-ma-**link**-ee) *noun* a jocular name for any very thin person or animal: *Is that boy of theirs still such a big skinnymalink?*

**skirlie** *noun* a dish of oatmeal and onions fried together, eaten either as a vegetable with meat dishes, or on its own with potatoes: *There's a choice of skirlie or neeps as a side course.*

**skite** *verb* **1** to slip or slide: *Watch ye don't skite on that icy pavement.* **2** to bounce rapidly from a surface: *My ball skited off the green and into the bunker; The hail was skitin' off the pavement.* | *noun* a glancing blow or slap: *You're askin' for a skite on the lug.* Someone who is **on the skite** is on a drunken spree: *staggering home after a night on the skite*

**skittery** *or* **skitterie** *adjective* fiddly and time-consuming: *It's a skittery job threading a needle.*

**skliff** *or* **scliff** *verb* to walk without lifting your feet properly, so that your shoes scrape along the ground: *If you don't stop that scliffing your good shoes'll need soled in no time.* | *noun* **1** the sound made by someone's shoes scraping along the ground as they walk: *She could hear the skliff of his boots in the close as he came wearily up the steps.* **2** a segment of something: *Gie's a skliff of your orange.*

**slàinte mhath** (*pronounced* **slan**-ja **vah**) *interjection* a Gaelic toast used especially when drinking whisky (often shortened to *slàinte*) [literally meaning good health]

**sleekit** (*pronounced* **slee**-kit) *adjective* outwardly charming and smooth, but actually untrustworthy and sly: *She's a sleekit two-faced besom.*

**sleuch** (*pronounced* **slooCH**) *or* **sluch** (*pronounced* **sluCH**) *verb* to drink noisily, usually from a spoon or through a straw: *Do you have to sleuch your soup like that?*

**slitter** *or* **slutter** *spoken in Central & South* *noun* a messy eater or drinker: *You've got pakora sauce all down your front, you slitter!* | *verb* to make a mess, especially by spilling or dribbling something: *Now, I want no sluttering on my good tablecloth.*

**slunge** *verb* to rinse something superficially by pouring water over it or dipping it into water: *I'll just slunge the mugs out under the tap.*

**smeddum** (*pronounced* **smed-dum**) *noun* an admirable mixture of determination, resourcefulness and common sense: *I like a lassie wi' a bit o' smeddum.* [Old English **smedema**]

**smirr** *noun* drizzly rain falling gently in small drops: *a smirr o' rain; There's a bit of a smirr outside.* | *verb* to rain in light drizzle: *It's been smirring all afternoon.*

**smowt** *or* **smout** *noun* **1** a small person, whether a child or undersized adult: *Ye're no feart fae that wee smowt?* **2** a young salmon or sea trout: *A smowt like this should be thrown back in.*

**snash** *noun* cheeky, impudent talk: *Ah'm no takin any snash fae the likes o' her!*

146

**sneck** *noun* a catch or latch on a door, gate etc: *Just lift the sneck and go in.* | *verb* to fasten a door, gate etc it with a catch or latch: *The coos'll no get oot if ye sneck the gate efter ye.*

**snell** *adjective* bitingly cold: *It's a snell wind that's blawin' aff the braes.* [Old English]

**snib** *noun* a bolt or catch on a door or window: *Put the snib on the front door before you go to bed.* | *verb* to lock a door or window using a snib: *The door'll no open; it must be snibbed on the inside.*

**snorl** *noun* spoken in Northeast an awkward situation, a scrape or predicament: *Whit a snorl ye've got yersel intil!* [from **snarl**]

**sonsie** or **sonsy** (*pronounced* **sonss**-ee)
*adjective* plump, cheerful-looking, and
attractive: *She was a big, braw, sonsie lass.*
[Gaelic **sonas** meaning good fortune]

**sook** or **souk** *verb* to suck: *The wean
was sookin' its dummy.* If you **sook
in** or **sook up** you are trying to curry
favour with someone by behaving
sycophantically: *You only get on here
if you're prepared to sook in to the boss.*
| *noun* **1** a suck: *Gie's a sook o' yer ice lolly.*
**2** someone who behaves sycophantically
towards their superiors; a crawler or
toady: *He sits through every meeting,
grinning and nodding like a total sook.*

**sooth-moother** (*pronounced* sooth-
**moodh**-er) *noun spoken in Shetland*
someone with an accent from a more

southerly area: *craft shops owned by sooth-moothers from Surrey and Knightsbridge*

> This term can be slightly derogatory. It depends who's saying it and to whom!

**souch** *or* **sough** (*pronounced* **sooCH**) *verb* usually referring to the wind, to blow or howl noisily: *There's aye a gey cold wind souching down King Street.* | *noun* the noise made by a strong wind: *lying in bed listening to the souch of the north wind in the birks* If you **keep a calm souch** you stay calm or quiet in a difficult situation, without panicking or becoming excited: *Keep a calm souch till the worst is ower, then we'll see what's what.* [Old English *swogan*]

**spaewife** (*pronounced* **spay**-wife) *noun* a woman who is supposed to be able to foretell the future: *Her pals dared her to go to the spaewife and have her fortune told.* [from the Old Norse]

**spaiver** *or* **spaver** (*pronounced* **spay**-ver) *noun spoken in East* the fly on a pair of trousers: *Pull up yer spaiver, it's at half-mast.*

**speir** (*pronounced* **speer**) *verb* to ask or inquire: *They speirt if I'd seen her.*

**spelk** *noun* a splinter of wood, especially one which has become embedded in your skin: *He got a spelk in his thumb.*

**speug** (*pronounced* **spyug**) *or* **spug** *noun* a sparrow: *A wee speug landed on the table and flew away with a crumb.*

**sploonging** (*pronounced* **sploon**-jing) *adjective* soaking wet, generally involving puddles of water: *Rain had been getting in through the roof, and the floor was sploonging.*

**sprauchle** (*pronounced* **sprawCH**-l) *or* **sprachle** (*pronounced* **spraCH**-l) *verb* to clamber or make your way slowly and with difficulty: *It took her nearly twenty minutes to sprauchle up the brae.*

**spurgie** (*pronounced* **sper**-gee) *noun spoken in Northeast* a sparrow: *We couldnae sleep for the chirpin' o' a nest o' spurgies.*

**stammygaster** (*pronounced* stam-mee-**gas**-ter) *spoken in Northeast noun* a shock or unpleasant surprise: *Ah never*

151

had such a *stammygaster!* | *verb* to give someone a shock or unpleasant surprise: *He was fair stammygastered by the news.*

**stank** *noun spoken in Central* **1** the gutter at the side of the road: *dead leaves lying in the stanks* **2** a drain at the side of a road, or the grating covering one: *He dropped a pound coin and watched in agony as it disappeared into a stank.* **Down the stank** means lost beyond all hope of retrieval: *That's mair money doon the stank at that bookies.*

**stappit** (*pronounced* **stap**-pit) *or* **stappit fu** *adjective* as full as it can possibly be: *Folk say that loch's stappit fu wi fish; Na, nae puddin for me. Ah'm stappit.*

**steamie** *noun spoken in Central &
Southern* an old-fashioned public
laundry where people took their clothes
and washed them themselves: *My
mother used to take her washing to the
steamie in an old pram.* Someone or
something that is **the talk of the steamie**
is very much gossiped about: *If you two
keep having lunch together you'll be the
talk of the steamie round here.*

**steen** *noun spoken in North* a stone:
*flingin' steens in the watter*

**stey** (*pronounced* **stie**) *adjective* steep
and difficult to get up: *a stey brae*

**stoat** *or* **stot** *verb* to bounce: *The rain
was stoatin off the pavement; She stoated
the ball off the ground.*

## Tartan talk

It's one of the quirks of history that the wearing of kilts and tartan has come to be so closely associated with Scottish identity. From shortbread tins to ladies' skirts, tartan is used everywhere to immediately declare Scottishness. The travelling support of the Scottish national football team is proud to call itself the Tartan Army, and many of them have taken to wearing forms of dress on their nether regions which can only vaguely be identified as kilts.

The fact is that there was never any such thing as 'Scottish national dress' and that tartans and kilts belong more properly to the culture of the Gaelic-speaking Highlands. People wearing kilts to attend a Burns night, for example, would be regarded as odd by the poet himself, who, as a Scots- and English-speaking Lowlander, would never have worn such garb himself.

Much is made, especially by members of the Scottish diaspora, of being entitled by one's surname to wear a particular pattern of tartan, but the idea of clan tartans was largely a product of the romanticization of Highland culture in the nineteenth century led by Sir Walter Scott. Before then, weavers in particular areas would often use a similar pattern and the colour would be decided by the natural dyes that were easiest to come by rather than clan identification.

However, after having been banned as part of the clampdown on Highland clans in the wake of the failed Jacobite Rebellion in 1746, tartan was given a new lease of life by the Georgian and Victorian love of all things Scottish.

**stoater** *noun* something or someone that is an outstanding or exceptional example of its kind: *McLean scored in the last minute with a stoater of a shot from twenty-five yards; See thon blonde lassie works up the stair? A right wee stoater, eh?*

**stoatin** *or* **stottin** *adjective* so drunk as to have difficulty walking without staggering: *He gets stoatin fou every Friday; Don't you dare come home stoatin again tonight.*

**stookie** *noun* 1 a plaster cast for a broken limb: *She came back from the hospital with a big stookie on her arm.* 2 someone who is ill-at-ease, out of place or unable to make conversation: *Nobody knew anybody else and we just sat* *there like a lot of stookies.* [a Scots form of **stucco**, meaning plaster of Paris, or a plaster statue]

**stooshie** *or* **stushie** *noun* a row or uproar, usually in protest: *Plans to redevelop the harbour area have raised a stooshie in the town; Ach, it's no worth making a stooshie about.*

**stotter** *verb* To stagger or stumble: *He went stotterin off down the road.*

**stour** *or* **stoor** (*pronounced* **stoor**) *noun* dust: *The place was full of stour after we cleared the bookshelves.*

**stourie** *or* **stoorie** (*pronounced* **stoo-ree**) *adjective* dusty: *It's awful stourie under that bed.*

**stramash** (*pronounced* stra-**mash**)
*noun* a disorderly commotion or
argument: *Two men were arrested
following a stramash in a city-centre
street in the early hours of Sunday
morning.*

**stravaig** (*pronounced* stra-**vayg**) *verb* to
wander or roam aimlessly: *It's all right
for you, stravaiging about the countryside,
but some of us have to work for a living.*
| *noun* a long, aimless ramble or
journey: *We just want to go from A to B,
not be sent on some daft stravaig all over
the place.* [from older Scots **extravage** to
wander]

**stroupach** (*pronounced* **stroop**-aCH)
*noun* *spoken in North* a drink of tea:
*Ye'll have time to come in for a stroupach?*

[from **stroup**, the mouth or spout of a kettle, pump, etc]

**sumph** *noun* a stupid, slow-witted person: *It's right in front of ye, ye muckle sumph!*

**swack** *adjective spoken in North* fit and supple: *I'm no so swack as I used to be.* [from Flemish]

**swatch** *noun* a look at something: *Gie's a swatch at your paper when you're finished wi' it.*

**swedger** (*pronounced* **swej**-er) *noun* a sweet, such as a mint, toffee or chocolate: *Pass the swedgers round, will you?*

**sweetiewife** (*pronounced* **swee**-ti-wife) *noun* a person, man or woman, who is very gossipy: *Mind yer ain business, ya pair o' auld sweetiewives!* [originally a woman who sells sweets]

> Apparently the sweetness of these ladies' wares was not reflected in their characters.

**sweir** (*pronounced* **sweer**) *adjective* unwilling or reluctant: *When it came tae hard work he wasnae sweir.* [from Old Northumbrian *swǣr* meaning lazy]

**swick** *verb* to cheat or swindle: *Aye, ye were swickit there.* | *noun* a swindle or swindler: *There was naethin in the box ava'. It was naethin' but a swick.*

**swither** *verb* to be unable to decide or choose: *The board is still swithering about investing many millions in a new*

ground or renovating the current
stadium. | noun a state of indecision:
I'm in a bit of a swither about what to
wear.

**syboes** (*pronounced* **sie**-beez) *plural
noun* spring onions: *Ah says tae the
lassie 'See's hauf a pun o' syboes, hen,' an'
she looks at us as if Ah wis speakin' double
Dutch.* [from French ***ciboule***]

**synd** *or* **syne** (*pronounced* **sine**) *verb* to
rinse something out or give it a quick
wash: *Synd oot thae dishes.* | *noun* a
rinse or quick wash: *Just gie yer cup a wee
synd an' we'll be off.*

**syne** (*pronounced* **sine**) *adverb* **1** since or
ago: *It's mair nor three years syne.* **2** then:
*Syne in comes ma mither.*

**syver** (*pronounced* **sie**-ver) *noun* a drain in a road, or the grating that covers it: *Frankie fun a fiver lyin' in the syver.*

**tackety** (*pronounced* **ta**-kit-ti) *adjective* referring to footwear, with hobnails or studs in the soles: *a decent pair of tackety boots with steel toecaps*

**tait** (*pronounced* **tayt**) *noun* a small piece or amount of something: *just a wee tait of sugar in my coffee*

**tak tent** *phrase* to pay heed to something, to take care: *It's no as easy as it looks, so tak tent.*

**tanner ba** *noun* literally, a ball costing sixpence (the pre-decimal equivalent of 2.5 pence). In Scottish football, part of the mythology of

the 'good old days' is that the best
players emerged from poverty, where
they learned their skills with no other
equipment than the cheapest of balls:
*The Lisbon Lions didnae have a' these
trainin facilities. A tanner ba was good
enough fur them.*

**tapsalteerie** (*pronounced* tap-sl-**tee**-
ree) *adjective, adverb* **1** upside-down:
*Sometimes I think the whole world's gone
tapsalteerie.* **2** untidy and chaotic, or in
an untidy and chaotic way: *Dirty clothes
were scattered tapsalteerie around the
room.*

**tattie** (*pronounced* **tat**-ee *or* **tot**-ee) *noun*
a potato: *mince and tatties; It's sair on yer
back, howkin tatties.*

## William Wallace

The Scottish patriot Sir William Wallace was born around 1270 and died in grisly fashion in 1305. His name was revered for centuries as an icon of the Scottish nationalist movement, but became globally known only after the blockbuster film *Braveheart* was released in 1995. The movie's Australian-American director and star (Mel Gibson) and its American writer (Randall Wallace, no relation) may be forgiven for, in the best Hollywood tradition of course, taking a few liberties with historical fact. However, there is a danger that their heavily romanticized version of Wallace's life could become accepted as truth when the reality was probably much different.

Much of what is taken as fact about Wallace's career actually springs from an epic poem written about him by a certain 'Blind Harry' almost two centuries after his death. Unlike his big-screen avatar, the real Wallace would not have been seen running around in a kilt with blue woad smeared all over his manly features and his rockstar locks blowing in the wind. He would have fought in chain mail or armour, usually on horseback, as befitted a son of the minor Lowland nobility.

He undoubtedly struck a great blow for Scottish freedom when, with powerful allies like Sir Andrew Murray, he achieved a crushing victory over the English at Stirling Bridge (1297). However, less than a year later, his forces were defeated by Edward I at Falkirk. He was betrayed to the English by a fellow Scot, Sir John Menteith, and, after a show trial, executed in London by being hung, drawn and quartered – a public spectacle popular at the time. Wallace became a figure of legend but for his actual achievements he does deserve a place in the nationalist pantheon.

**tattie-bogle** (*pronounced* **tat**-ee-**boe**-gl) *noun* a scarecrow: *He was in old ragged clothes like a tattie-bogle.*

**tattie-boodie** *noun spoken in Northeast* a scarecrow: *standing out in the field like a tattie-boodie*

**tee-name** *noun spoken in Northeast* a nickname: *Everybody knew him as Zorba, for that was his tee-name in the Merchant Service.*

**telt** *verb* the past tense of tell; told: *Ah've no seen it, Ah telt ye.*

**teuch** (*pronounced* **chooCH** *or* **chuCH**) *adjective* tough and hard to chew: *This steak's a bit teuch.*

**teuchat** (*pronounced* **chooCH**-it) *noun*

*spoken in Eastern* a lapwing: *The only sound was the cry of a teuchat high over the field.* [imitating the bird's call]

**teuchter** (*pronounced* **chooCH**-ter) *noun* a Lowland name for a Highlander, especially a Gaelic-speaking one: *They put up bilingual street signs in Airdrie so that the teuchters down for the Mod could find their way around; a pub frequented by Glasgow's teuchter community*

> Many people think of this term as harmless and chiefly affectionate, but as some Highlanders consider it to be derogatory it should only be used with care among strangers.

**thae** (*pronounced* **dhey**) *determiner*
those: *Post thae letters for me, will ye?*

**thirled** *adjective* bound to something by
obligation, duty or habit: *Scottish public-
sector workers are thirled to the British
state which pays their wages.*

**thrang** *adjective* busy, meaning both
crowded with people and fully
occupied doing something: *streets
thrang with shoppers; I'm ower thrang
to help.*

**thrapple** *noun* the throat or windpipe:
*Get this doon yer thrapple.*

**thraw** *verb spoken in East* to twist or
sprain a joint or limb: *I've thrawed my
ankle.*

**thrawn** *adjective* awkward and obstinate, often taking delight in being difficult and uncooperative: *That thrawn old devil would argue black was white; a thrawn inability to agree about anything important*

**through-other** *adjective* untidy, disordered or dishevelled: *The place is just a through-other mess.*

**toorie** *noun* a round bobble or pompom on a hat: *A woolly hat's not complete without a braw toorie on the top.* A **toorie bunnet** is a hat with a bobble on it, especially a knitted bobble-hat: *Here's a picture of Tom Weir in his toorie bunnet at the top of Goat Fell.* [from **toor**, the Scots form of **tower**]

**torn-faced** *adjective* *spoken in Central* having a bad-tempered or grumpy expression: *What's she looking so torn-faced about now?*

**totie** (*pronounced* **toe**-tee) *or* **tottie** (*pronounced* **tot**-ee) *adjective* very small: *a totie wee baby*

**tottie** *or* **totty** (*pronounced* **tot**-ee) *spoken in West Central.* *same as* **tattie**

**towsie** *adjective* rough and bad-tempered: *It was a towsie relegation battle with no goals but plenty of bookings.*

> The word is especially used to describe a game of football or rugby in which there is little flowing play and many petty (or not-so-petty) fouls.

**trauchle** (*pronounced* **trawCH**-l) *or*
**trachle** (*pronounced* **traCH**-l) *noun*
hard work, usually monotonous and
unrewarding: *It took years of hard*
*trauchle before he saw any success.* | *verb*
**1** to walk or work slowly and wearily:
*She trauchled up the brae with her bags*
*of messages; trauchling away at a job he*
*hated* **2** to tire out or exhaust, especially
by long hard work: *Make us a cup o' tea.*
*Ah'm sair trauchled after comin up a' thae*
*stairs.*

**tumshie** (*pronounced* **tum**-shee) *noun*
*spoken in Central & South* a turnip: *She*
*got a casual job lifting tumshies.*

**unco** (*pronounced* **ung**-ka) *adjective*
**1** very or extremely: *The island has*
*a whisky trail for the unco drouthy.*

171

**2** strange or unfamiliar: *an unco sicht*
**Unco guid** means excessively religious,
self-righteous, or narrow-minded.: *Is
Gaeldom populated exclusively by drunks
and the unco guid?* [a Scottish variant of
**uncouth**]

> One of Burns's best-known
> poems is the 'Address to the
> Unco Guid', an attack on the
> rigidly righteous.

**vennel** (*pronounced* **ven**-l) *noun* a lane
or alley: *We went on a ghost walk through
the vennels of Edinburgh's Old Town.*
[from French]

**voe** *noun spoken in Orkney & Shetland* a
small bay or narrow creek (often found
in place names): *The Isle of Balta all but*

172

*fills the mouth of the voe; Sullom Voe*
[Old Norse]

**vratch** *noun spoken in Northeast* a
despicable or pitiable person: *Ah'm
scunnered wi' her behaviour, the dirty
vratch!* [a form of **wretch**]

**wabbit** (*pronounced* **wab**-bit) *adjective*
tired, run down, and lacking in energy: *I
think I'll have an early night: I'm feeling a
bit wabbit.*

**wallie** *or* **wally** (*pronounced* **wal**-li)
*adjective* made of porcelain or glazed
china: *She had the regulation pair of
wallie dugs on the mantelpiece.*

> In the late nineteenth and
> early twentieth century, a
> pair of decorative china

dogs or 'wallie dugs' was a standard feature of Scottish living rooms. In twenty-first century, however, most Scots would no longer regard these as a desirable feature.

**waur** (*pronounced* **war**) *adjective* worse: *I'd be nane the waur o' a long lie in the mornin'.*

**wean** (*pronounced* **wayn**) *noun spoken in West Central* a child, especially a young one: *Try that if you have four weans and a fat lazy husband; an exchange scheme involving local weans and some pupils from Germany* [a contraction of *wee ane* little one]

**Weedgie** (*pronounced* **wee**-jee) *noun* a derogatory Edinburgh name for anybody from Glasgow: *Why build a new stadium on the outskirts where it will be easier for Weedgies to get to than the club's own supporters?* [a shortening of **Glaswegian**]

**weel** *adjective, adverb* well: *He's no awfy weel; He's no weel aff; Take yer wee brither as weel.*

**weel-kent** (*pronounced* weel-**kent**) *adjective* well known or familiar: *These are weel-kent names to Scotland's real-ale drinkers; Now, there's a weel-kent face!*

**wersh** *adjective* having an unpleasant taste, whether through being too bland or sour: *Soup made with water rather than stock can be gey wersh; The strawberries were still under-ripe and wersh.*

## A tale of two cities

Much is made of the animosity that is said to exist between Scotland's two largest cities, Glasgow and Edinburgh. Certainly, there are reasons for friction between them. Glasgow is the larger, but Edinburgh is the capital and the seat of the Scottish Parliament. On the other hand, if Edinburgh supporters of the Scottish national football team wish to support their heroes at home games they have to travel west, as the national stadium, Hampden Park, is in Glasgow.

The physical distance between the two places is not vast. Three-quarters of an hour by train, an hour by bus, a little more by car – given the volume of traffic on the M8 and both city centres' growing antipathy to private vehicles – will take you from one to the other. But perhaps the distance is greater in terms of attitude than it is in mileage.

Glaswegians are given to describing the capital as 'aw fur coat an nae knickers', implying that the outward appearance of being affluent is all-important, even to the point of skimping on skimpies. They also claim that visitors to a Glasgow household will be offered refreshment, while in Edinburgh the host is more likely to greet guests with 'You'll have had your tea.'

In Edinburgh, Glaswegians may be contemptuously dismissed as 'weegies', and associated with poverty, violence, and drunkenness. However, you don't have to read all of Ian Rankin's *Rebus* novels to know that Edinburgh is not immune from these vices itself.

Nowadays this rivalry is pretty much a myth, but one that is encouraged for the sake of mutual mickey-taking and sparking the interest of visitors.

**whaup** (*pronounced* **whawp**) *noun* a curlew: *the plaintive cry of a whaup on the muir* [imitation of the bird's cry]

**wheech** (*pronounced* **wheeCH**) *verb* to move quickly: *He went wheeching down the hill on his bike; The barman tried to wheech my pint away before I'd finished.* [imitation of the sound of something moving rapidly through the air]

**wheen** *determiner* an indeterminate but reasonably large number or quantity: *There's still a wheen of work to do.*

**wheesht** *or* **wheesh** *interjection* be quiet!: *Wheesht till Ah hear this announcement!* | *verb* to tell someone to be quiet: *parents wheeshting their children* | *noun* **Haud your wheesht** means to be

quiet: *Would you pair haud your wheesht!
Yer argy-bargyin's giein me a headache.*

**whigmaleerie** (*pronounced* whig-ma-**lee**-ree) *noun* a decoration, trinket, or ornament: *the whigmaleeries and curlie-wurlies of statuettes which adorn the monument*

**widdershins** (*pronounced* **wid**-er-shinz) *or* **withershins** (*pronounced* **widh**-er-shinz) *adverb* anti-clockwise or in a direction opposite to the course of the sun: *He made a circling motion widdershins in the air.* [from a Middle High German word meaning opposite course, from ***wider*** against plus ***sin*** course]

> Widdershins is traditionally
> seen as the opposite way

from normal, and among
the superstitious to do
something widdershins is
thought to bring bad luck.

**wyle** *spoken in Northeast* *verb* to choose:
*Ye can wyle yer pick.* | *noun* a choice
or selection: *a wyle o' twa hooses* **The**
**wyle** is the best or choice example of
something: *She could tak her pick frae the*
*wyle o' them.*

**wynd** *noun* a narrow street or lane, often
a winding one, which leads off a larger
or more important street: *the wynds,*
*courts, and closes of the Royal Mile*

**yestreen** (*pronounced* yes-**treen**) *adverb*
last night, or sometimes, more loosely,
yesterday: *It was gey wet yestreen.* [a

contraction of **yester-**, as in yesterday, plus **even** evening]

**yett** *noun* a gate: *the prison yett; as daft as a yett on a windy day*

> In place names such as **the Yetts o' Muckhart**, a **yett** is a pass running between hills.

**yin** *noun* one: *Let's see the ither yin again; Youse yins will have tae wait.*

**yirdit** *adjective spoken in Northeast* dirty: *The bairn was yirdit wi' glaur.* [from **yird**, a Scots word for earth]

**yoke** *verb spoken in Northeast* to start work for the day (or shift): *Are you no yokit yet?*

**yowe** *noun* a female adult sheep, a ewe: *a park o' breedin yowes wi' lambs*

## Suggestions for Further Reading

*The Scottish Islands*: Hamish Haswell-Smith (Canongate)

*Tracing Your Scottish Ancestors*: Cecil Sinclair (Mercat Press)

*Oxford Dictionary of First Names*: Patrick Hanks & Flavia Hodges (OUP)

*Scottish Place Names*: WFH Nicolaisen (Batsford)

*Scottish Place Names*: David Ross (Birlinn)

*Scottish Surnames*: George Mackay (Lomond Books)

*Bumper Book Of Babies Names*: Jacqueline Harrod & Andre Page (Clarion)

*Collins Guide to Scots Kith & Kin* (Harper Collins)

*Scottish Surnames*: David Dorward (Mercat Press)

*Scotland's Place Names*: David Dorward (Mercat Press)

*Clans & Tartans*: James MacKay (Lomond Books)

*Scottish First Names*: George MacKay (Lomond Books)

*Scottish Christian Names*: Leslie Alan Dunkling (Johnson & Bacon)

*Illustrated Encyclopedia of Scotland*: edited Iseabail MacLeod (Lomond Books)

*Collins Encyclopedia of Scotland*: John & Julia Keay (Harper Collins)

*Surnames of Scotland*: George F. Black (Birlinn)

*Scottish Place Names* (Harper Collins)

*Scottish Names* (Harper Collins)